D1261757

3
RESPONSIBILITY FOR CRIME

STUDIES IN HISTORY, ECONOMICS AND PUBLIC LAW

EDITED BY THE FACULTY OF POLITICAL SCIENCE OF
COLUMBIA UNIVERSITY

Volume XXXIV]   [Number 3

Whole Number 91

RESPONSIBILITY FOR CRIME

An Investigation of the Nature and Causes of Crime and a Means of its Prevention

BY

PHILIP A. PARSONS

AMS PRESS
NEW YORK

COLUMBIA UNIVERSITY
STUDIES IN THE
SOCIAL SCIENCES

91

The Series was formerly known as
Studies in History, Economics and Public Law.

Reprinted with the permission of Columbia University Press
From the edition of 1909, New York
First AMS EDITION published 1968
Manufactured in the United States of America

Library of Congress Catalogue Card Number: 75-76683

AMS PRESS, INC.
NEW YORK, N. Y. 10003

PREFACE

THE following dissertation is the outcome of a three years' study of the subject of crime in all its phases on the general basis of Professor Giddings' explanation of society as a product of like response to stimuli. A study of the works of the so-called "Italian School" of Criminal Anthropologists and of those of their foremost American contemporaries resulted in the working-out of the writer's own theories in regard to crime and the criminal set forth herein. Owing to the widespread aversion to the subject in general, a special effort has been made to present it in as popular phraseology as possible, under the impression that reforms can come only as a result of a general understanding of the situation in the minds of the people. This effort accounts for a notable lack of scientific expression in the work, popular terms being substituted for technical ones wherever possible. The works of Lombroso and Maudsley have been of exceptional value, as have those of E. Ferri, Havelock Ellis and Dr. Drähms. Special thanks are due to Dr. Giddings for his kindly interest.

It is the author's ambition to enlarge upon the present text in a still more popular and comprehensive form at some future time.

P. A. P.

COLUMBIA UNIVERSITY, MAY, 1909.

ERRATA

Page 99, line 14. For "degredation" read "degradation."

Page 101, lines 2 and 3 from the bottom, omit quotation marks from "*New Jersey Review of Charities and Corrections*."

Page 119, line 7, after the word "consideration" insert "*only*."

Page 119, line 17. For "potent" read "patent."

Page 155, 4th paragraph, 2d line. For "detention" read "detection."

Page 178, 2d paragraph, line 6. For "individuality" read "individual responsibility."

Page 176, insert in line 12 after "by" the words: "or at the instigation of."

CONTENTS

CHAPTER IV

Punishment

Idea complex—Personal vengeance—Present day purpose—The interests of society—Early punishment instinctive—Punishment transformed or disguised vengeance—Not moral—Must be abandoned—Preventive—Does not deter—Value negative—The interests of the criminal—Responsibility and free will—The extenuating circumstance—Rise of statistics—Response to stimuli—Moral freedom of little consequence...................... 56

CHAPTER V

Heredity and Environment

The criminal personality—Its surroundings—The attempt to determine relative influence futile—Heredity and the criminal classes —Nature of heredity—Alcoholism—Evidence of hereditary taint—Criminal families—Tribe of Ishmael—The Owens—The Jukes—Play of environment—In classes—Slums due to great social laws—Real scope of environment—Importance of heredity—Tarde's conjectures—Problem not to be solved by a little readjustment—Criminality synchronous with struggle for existence and progress—Amount can be greatly lessened.......... 70

CHAPTER VI

The Death Penalty

Origin of practice—Barbarous custom—Retributive idea an outgrowth of religion—Deterrent idea—Gradual decrease in practice—McKim's scheme—Altruism—Benefits to society—Origin of humanity—History of humane instinct—Violation of law of survival—Inconsistencies of its abnormal products.............. 84

CHAPTER VII

The Prison System

Esteem of personal liberty—Prison not associated with crime at first—Cannibalism and religion—Motives for taking captives— First prisons—Early appearance in England—History—Progress —Corruption— Present motives—Generally condemned—The evil effects of short sentences—Luxurious prisons and their influence—Prisons to be abandoned—The substitute........... 95

CONTENTS

CHAPTER VIII

The Jury

CHAPTER IX

Justice and Restitution

CHAPTER X

Propagation

CHAPTER XI

A Remedy

CHAPTER XII

EDUCATION

CHAPTER XIII

PROGRESS

CHAPTER XIV

RETROSPECT AND PROSPECT

CHAPTER I

CRIME AND THE CRIMINAL

"ORDER in the court!" The judge's gavel falls and every one in the crowded room bends forward in apprehension. Facing the learned justice stands a shivering wretch whom a jury "of his peers" has declared to be "guilty as charged." In the midst of a tense silence, the sentence is imposed and the face of the trembling prisoner at the bar turns a shade paler than usual as he clutches the rail to keep from falling. "Hard labor for life. Officer, remove the prisoner."

This familiar and oft-repeated scene is the consummation of a long series of incidents, each trivial in itself but potent in connection with the others. An unkind fate has forged the last link in a long chain reaching back into the ages. Can it be possible that any link is an accident? Or has the whole been forged under the ruthless hammer of destiny? Why the court and the "jury of peers," and why the "criminal at the bar?" Can it be possible that the court and the jury are the result of a long-acting evolution and the criminal and his crime not? What constitutes crime, and why is it committed? Why is the man separated from his fellows, and why the "hard labor for life?"

Social relationships have been disrupted and are still disturbed by three forms of human conduct varying from the normal. They and the normal shade into each other almost imperceptibly, yet each association of men is called upon to make a distinction between them and the normal, and does so in a more or less crude and arbitrary fashion. These abnormal forms of conduct are sin, tort, and crime. Sin has to do with individual action as conforming or not conforming to a certain code of ethics or morals held by the individual himself. It need not concern any other being and hence is not necessarily an anti-social act. The field of sin changes with the changing of the moral code. " If I had not come you would not have sinned, but now that I have come you have no excuse for your sin."

A tort is essentially a private injury as distinguished from a public wrong. It is a harm inflicted by a man upon his fellow-man not regarded as a wrong done the state, but giving rise to a civil suit for damages. In ancient times the injured man might have sought private vengeance and a blood feud might have resulted. Later it became customary to accept arbitration and pecuniary composition. Society gave to this arbitration a legal form and made the acceptance of the damages awarded compulsory, unless the plaintiff chose not to press his suit. Thus, for a tribesman to kill or steal from a man of another clan within his own tribe was a tort demanding vengeance or compensation.[1]

Tort is partly individual, partly social, having to do with the individual rights of associates. Sin may pass over into crime, tort never does. " Sin is personal, crime is civil. Sin is a violation of the individual conscience; crime is a challenge to the social order. One is an enlarged expression of the other. The first sin was against Deity; the first crime was against man's brother." [2]

Crime is that action or lack of action which in some way

[1] Hall, *Crime and Social Progress*, p. 16.
[2] Drähms, *The Criminal*, p. 5.

violates not only the moral code or the individual rights but also violates the code which safeguards the interests of the whole social group. It is entirely a social action, or better, an anti-social action. Sin becomes crime when the moral code violated has become the established code of a majority of the group.

In spite of the common belief that what is once a crime is always a crime and that there is a sort of criterion of rightness and wrongness by which all men in all ages are bound, we find that the amount and nature of crime are never static. This fact was recognized and stated by Beccaria nearly a hundred and fifty years ago.

Whosoever reads with a philosophic eye the history of nations and their laws will generally find that the ideas of virtue and vice, of a good or a bad citizen, change with the revolution of ages. He will frequently observe that the passions and vice of one age are the foundation of the morality of the following; that violent passion, the offspring of fanaticism, and enthusiasm being weakened by time, which reduces all the phenomena of the natural and moral world to an equality, become, by degrees the prudence of the age.[1]

Crimes change with the changing of ideas or customs and actions which once roused a whole populace into a fenzy of protest, may not cause, in a subsequent generation, a quickened pulse beat in a single individual. The average American reads without mental comment of the multiple matrimonial relations of David and Solomon, but is horrified at a description of a modern Turkish harem. For the American, the Semitic custom has long since disappeared, with the exception of a belated trace at Utah; for the Turk it survives in all its ancient lust and splendor to this day.

[1] *Essay on Crime*, ch. iv.

Crime, then, in the broadest meaning of the term, is any infraction of established or codified custom or public sentiment at a given moment.

We see readily how an action which would constitute a crime in one social group might be a legitimate and even honorable action in another. The savage kills his enemy with pleasure but is restrained from doing bodily harm to his kindred; the religious fanatic thinks that he is doing God a service by torturing, maltreating, or even putting to death that member of his own group or even household who holds heretical opinions about the nature of God or refuses to believe in him in the same manner as himself. Some of the most bloody wars in history as well as some of the foulest crimes have been perpetrated in the name of law which was supposed to have been founded upon the teachings of the Man of Peace.

Grave concern is felt at present at what appears to be a rapid increase in the number of crimes committed in proportion to the increase of population. This alarm is expressed by Havelock Ellis in the following significant paragraph:

These problems, *i. e.,* those presented by the criminal situation, are becoming every day more pressing. The level of criminality, it is well known, is rising and has been rising during the whole of the present century (1800) throughout the civilized world. In France, Germany, Italy, Belgium, Spain, and the United States the tide of criminality is becoming higher steadily and rapidly. In France it has risen several hundred per cent; so also for several kinds of serious crime in many parts of Germany; in Spain the number of persons sent to imprisonment nearly doubled between 1870 and 1883; in the United States the criminal population has increased during thirty years relatively to the population by one-third.[1]

[1] *The Criminal,* p. 369.

Opposed to this we have the statement of Dr. Drähms that, while there is an immense increase in the amount of crime the greater part of it consists of petty offences; the graver forms tend to remain stationary or even to decrease in some foreign countries.[1] Hall's study of the history of crime among the English-speaking peoples tends very much to support this position. That crime has increased till now this work will give the evidence, so far, at least, as the English people are concerned. But the nature of crime has changed and will continue to change, from more to less heinous offences, if we may judge from the standpoint of present public opinion. Under the rule of law men have learned to curb their hasty passions. Crimes of force show a very great decrease during the last few centuries, and they are decreasing still.[2] The increase of crime, says Drähms, has been the prolific theme, alike on the part of pessimist and optimist, both of whom generally approach its oracular altars with " prejudice aforethought," and shape their conclusions in accordance therewith.[3] Hall's conclusions are probably very nearly correct, that, while crime is increasing in amount it is decreasing in intensity, that the great bulk of the increasing criminality is composed of petty or minor offences and that the graver forms of crime tend to decrease.

That the present state of criminality is due, in a large measure, to economic conditions cannot well be denied. Criminality, writes Ellis, like insanity, waits upon civilization. Among primitive races insanity is rare; criminality in the true sense is also rare. Conservatism and rigid cult of custom form as distinct a barrier against crime as they do against progressive civilization. As the methods of en-

[1] *The Criminal*, ch. x.   [2] *Crime and Social Progress*, ch. i.
[3] *The Criminal*, p. 239.

larging and multiplying the uses of our lives increase, so do the abuses of those methods.[1]

As the struggle for existence becomes more rigorous and wants and desires increase, the law of survival works with increasing rigor and cruelty. The mentally or physically strong, taking advantage of the increased opportunity for satisfaction of wants or gratification of desires, slowly but surely advance the standard of living. In the struggle to maintain their old standard or to keep pace with the new, the physically or mentally weak slowly but surely fall behind, or maintain the standard at the expense of vital wants and the exhaustion of nervous constitutions. As a result of this mal-nutrition and nervous exhaustion we soon have a large class born into the world much less fortunately equipped, either mentally or physically, than their parents to maintain their social position. A large number of these perish, falling an easy prey to disease; still another large portion of them become vagrants or dependents and fill our asylums, reformatories, and poor-houses; while the remainder either fall naturally into criminality or, filled with sullen anger at the society which exacts of them a standard of conduct which they are incapable of maintaining, turn upon their supposed oppressor and prey upon it. This group, augmented by the degenerate offspring of the debauched superior class, constitutes our criminal population. Thus crime is, in a large measure, the result of the activity of the social wreckage which floats miserably along in the wake of progress.

On the other hand, the present high rate of criminality may be partly accounted for by the enlarged field of legislation. As public sentiment becomes more and more sensitive, from whatever causes, the field of conduct offensive to it likewise increases. For instance, when science in the

[1] *The Criminal*, p. 370.

field of hygienics has educated a population to the extent of making spitting upon sidewalks or in public conveyances a misdemeanor, the otherwise honest and law-abiding but careless spitter becomes a malefactor. On a more grave scale, criminality has been enhanced in one direction at the same time that it has been decreased in others by prohibition laws making the sale of intoxicating beverages a crime. A yet more notable instance may be cited in the fact that, by large groups of highly respected people, smuggling is looked upon as an entirely moral act.

The increase of criminality from this source is no cause for alarm. It is the activity, in a large measure, of a portion of the population that is no real menace to society but which has not kept pace with the law-making portion in culture and refinement. On the other hand it may be caused by the codifying of certain ideas of reform which are held by barely enough of a population to constitute a legal majority, which leaves the remainder of the group bound by no other restraint than a rather vague loyalty to their institutions. On the whole, this phase of criminality is a sort of secondary evidence of moral progress which enlarges the field of restraint. In our own country, numerous subdivisions and refinements of the penal code are constantly going on, and petty misdemeanors today become penal offences tomorrow. In some of the states of the Union, the penal codes reach four and five hundred statutory provisions where but a few years ago they were limited to one-half or one-third of that number. The German code enumerates about 200 crimes and offences; the Italian 180 (the new code 200) ; and the French code about 150. All this materially enlarges the scope and current of contemporary criminality, and gives it an apparent weightiness and meaning hardly warranted by the real facts in the case.[1]

[1] Drähms, *The Criminal*, p. 267.

Again, the present apparent increase in criminality is in a large measure due to recidivation, criminal repetition— which is the ear mark of the instinctive criminal. Relapse, says Drähms, is the distinguishing peculiarity of the genuine criminal everywhere. The natural instincts and predisposing bent of the congenital and habitual offenders are instinctively toward repeatedly transgressional acts as the legitimate outcome of the criminal propensity.[1] In the United States the total number of recidivists by the census report of 1890 was 26.42 per cent of all prisoners. Drähms gives the following figures for foreign countries:

Country.	Year.	Percentage.	Year.	Percentage.
England	71-77	40	97	56
France	72	41	95	41
Austria	72-75	17	91-95	28
Wurtemberg	72	50	97	60
Belgium	72	46	98	39
Holland	72	80	97	44
All Europe (average).				50-60

This high proportion of recidivism in Europe as compared with that of the United States may be accounted for by the fact of the emigration of a large portion of the prospective criminal population to this country, which has a tendency to lower the number of first offenders in Europe and increase it in America.

The period between the ages of 25 and 35 seems to be the age of recidivism. The maximum of offences is usually reached at the first repetition. Thus from the Commissioner's report of the English Prisons (1897) we find first relapses numbered 21,056; second 10,866; third, 7,371; fourth, 5,526; fifth, 4,365; *etc.*

Old offenders sometimes attain high preëminence in

---

[1] Drähms, *The Criminal*, p. 222.

criminal degrees, thus in Germany 32 men and 16 women had been imprisoned 31 or more times; and 644 men and 163 women, from 11 to 30 times. The Scottish statistics give instances of 119 persons who had been convicted previously from 150 to 200 times; 154 who had been convicted previously 101 to 150 times; and 1,125 who had been so convicted 51 to 100 times.[1]

The process of criminal-making is constantly going on; nor are the social and economic conditions alone responsible for the criminality of a population. There is a wide range of factors which enter into the process, and to leave any factor out of consideration would be to decrease materially the value of an investigation. Ferri gives a statement of these based upon the assumption that human actions, whether honest or dishonest, social or anti-social, are always the outcome of man's physio-psychical organism, and of the physical and social atmosphere which surrounds him. He draws attention to the anthropological or individual factors of crime, the physical factors and the social factors.

The anthropological factors, inherent in the individual criminal, are the first conditions of crime; and they may be divided into three sub-classes, according as we regard the criminal organically, physically, or socially.

The organic constitution of the criminal comprises all anomalies of the skull, the brain, the vital organs, the sensibility, and the reflex activity, and all the bodily characteristics taken together, such as the physiognomy, tattooing, and so on.

The mental constitution of the criminal comprises anomalies of intelligence and feeling, especially of the moral sense, and the specialties of criminal writing and slang.

The personal characteristics of the criminal comprise his purely-biological conditions, such as race, age, sex; bio-social conditions, such as civil status, profession, domicile, social rank, instruction, education, which have hitherto been regarded as almost the exclusive concern of criminal statistics.

[1] *Report*, 1897, p. 81.

The physical factors of crime are climate, the nature of the soil, the relative length of day and night, the seasons, the average temperature, meteoric conditions, and agricultural pursuits.

The social factors comprise the density of population; public opinion, manners, and religion; alcoholism; economic and political conditions; public administration, justice and police; and in general, legislative, civil and penal institutions.[1]

No crime, continues Ferri, whoever commits it and in whatever circumstances, can be explained except as the outcome of individual free will, or as the natural effect of natural causes. Since the former of these explanations has no scientific value, it is impossible to give a scientific explanation of crime unless it is considered as the product of a particular organic and physical constitution, acting in a particular physical and social environment.[2]

At the conclusion of his chapter on the Demography of Crime, Dr. Drähms states the situation admirably in regard to the increase or decrease of criminality.

A question as to whether crime is on the increase or on the decrease is, on the whole, about as unsatisfactory as that other form of the inquiry; Is the world growing better or worse? . . . The foundation principles of human nature remain practically unchanged. Men function from the same impulsions to-day, yesterday, and forever. The sources of all responsible conduct are inseparably interwoven with the personality. Crime is its social culmination. The moral cause of the catastrophe goes further back than any mere social or judicial remedies can reach. We do not expect crime to cease in this sense; it only changes expression. We can mitigate, we cannot cure.[3]

[1] *Criminal Sociology*, p. 52.   [2] *Ibid.*, p. 54.
[3] *The Criminal*, p. 269.

Nor is this conclusion pessimistic as it may, at first glance, appear. Until progress, social progress, ceases to produce the criminal classes we cannot hope for the cessation of criminality. On the other hand, moral progress must ever bring with it its accompaniment of law-breaking. How to reduce the criminality produced in this twofold manner to its smallest possible proportions in each succeeding generation will be the problem of the criminologist of the future. Toward the solutions of this problem, this volume is offered as a feeble yet hopeful contribution.

Since we have concluded that crime is any infraction of established or codified custom or public sentiment, the criminal is any one who commits this infraction. In other words, the criminal is a person who commits crime. Quetelet said, " The criminal is the instrument that executes crime." Thus far all is clear, but our problem is yet to be stated. Given your criminal—your person who commits crime—the all-engrossing question is why is he a criminal and from what source does he come? Why does he commit crime? Why does one man commit crime and not another? These are the questions that have forced themselves upon students of criminality. In want of an answer to them our penal machinery goes blundering on, in many cases trying with a broom to stem the tides of the sea. Until these questions are answered, all reforms must be in the nature of experiments, as at present all effort to deal with the situation is comparatively groping in the dark. The criminal is with us. In spite of our most ingenuous efforts he preys upon us. The most elaborate precautions of our modern civilization are inadequate to stop his depredations. We punish, we detain, we slay. By hundreds and by thousands we exterminate his kind but he reappears and in ever-increasing numbers ere we have rested from our labors of extermination.

Careful scientific study of such criminals as have fallen into the hands of the law has produced remarkable results. By such study it has been discerned that in a certain sense the criminal is a being apart; that by certain physical and mental characteristics he conforms more or less nearly to a sort of norm which Lombroso recognized and characterized as the Criminal Type.[1] To attain these results elaborate statistical investigations, covering a long period of years have been carried on by the French and Italian schools. In spite of the fact that Lombroso's conclusions have been severely criticized and are at present somewhat in disrepute, he and his disciples and even his critics have pretty generally established the fact that the criminal class is characterized by certain mental and physical characteristics to a far greater extent than a normal population. In considering Lombroso's theories, however, one must ever keep in mind a warning which he himself repeats again and again, —that the appearance of a greater or less number of these criminal characteristics in an individual does not prove his criminality; but, in a very high percentage of cases, when you have your criminal he presents these anomalies to a very high degree. Probably the best presentation and the most conservative criticism of his methods and conclusions may be found in the writings of Havelock Ellis and Dr. Drähms. To give a detailed description of the numerous characteristics of the criminal class with statistical matter to substantiate their claims to scientific proof would take many times the space allotted to this division of our subject and would only be retraversing the ground already well covered by comparatively recent works. It will be sufficient for our purposes to mention them with brief discussion of the most interesting and conclusive ones.

[1] *L'Homme criminel.*

Popular opinion has ever pictured the criminal as of repulsive appearance. In art and fiction we meet him presented in most forbidding forms. Criminal Anthropology has revealed the fact that popular opinion has not been far wrong. As a class the criminal as pictured by the " Italian" school presents a gruesome spectacle. His malformed head, either too large or too small, with many unexpected extensions or depressions, contains a brain defective in structure and function. An examination of it reveals an inferiority of form and histological type, as well as in the greater number of cases, indications of diseases which were frequently undetected during life. Facial asymmetry is the rule, not the exception. The eyes are too large or too small, too far apart or too close together, usually out of alignment with the rest of the features and, in a large number of cases, defective. The nose is different, many times enormous and protruding, sometimes diminutive and *retroussé,* nearly always crooked. The jaws are enormous with the exception of a few cases where there is underdevelopment, a case popularly known as " chinless." The ears are at once interesting and repellant, nearly always protruding and large, frequently without lobes and sometimes without the outer rim. In other instances the lobe is pendulous and again adhering to the cheek as far down as the base of the jaw bone. The hair is usually dark and coarse, in females inclining to be curly; many of the men have no beard.

Because of characteristic wrinkles the criminal early has the appearance of being prematurely old. Looking over the plates of Byrnes' book *Professional Criminals in America,* one is struck with the persistence of this trait. Criminal characteristics are evident to the most casual observer while the accompanying records show that out of 573 males 214 were tattooed, over 37%. Of the 18 women none were tattooed. The designs most popular were dancing girls and ships or anchors; in one case shown by Lombroso in the Atlas to *L'Homme criminel,* among many other designs, a nude woman and a crucifix were found on the same individual. Speaking of this trait Lombroso says: " Certainly one can say of the latter (tatooing) as of all other characteristics of criminals, that one can meet it among normal people; but it is the proportion, the diffusion, and the intensity which are indeed more salient; it is the specific shade, * * * the useless imprudent vanity of crime which are lacking among honest people and even among fools tatooing is very rare." [1]

As a class criminals are held to be physically weak and short lived. They are everywhere incapable of prolonged and sustained exertion; an amount of regular work which would ordinarily exhaust the most vigorous and rebellious would be easily accomplished by an ordinary workman; they are essentially idle; the whole art of crime lies in the endeavor to avoid the necessity of labor. The French criminals call themselves *pégres* (idle). Ellis cites the case of a philanthropic gentleman of Paris who offered employment of various kinds with payment of four francs a day to all who came to him complaining of hunger and complaining that they could get no work. Out of 727, 545 did not even present themselves; some came and disappeared after the first half-day, having claimed their two francs; only 18, or one out of forty, continued to work. [2]

According to the report of the Anthropometric Committee of the British Association (1883), industrial school boys of the age of 14 were nearly seven inches shorter of stature and 24¾ pounds lighter in weight than juveniles of the same age in the general English population.

---

[1] *L'Anthropologie criminelle*, p. 91.   [2] *Op. cit.,* pp. 167, 270.

Insensibility to pain has been found to be characteristic of criminals as well as inability to blush.

Dr. Harris, formerly corresponding secretary of the New York Prisons Association, after an inspection of the prisons of the state, in a paper on the relation of drunkenness to crime, says,

As a physician familiar with the morbid consequences of alcoholic indulgence in thousands of sufferers from it, it was easy for the writer to believe that not less than one-half of all crimes and pauperism in the state depends upon inebriety. But after two years of careful inquiry into the conditions of the criminal population of the state, I find that the conclusion is inevitable that, taken in all its relations, alcoholic drinks may be charged with far more than half of the crimes that are brought to conviction in the state of New York, and that full 85 per cent of all convicts give evidence of having in some larger degree been prepared or enticed to do criminal acts because of the physical and distracting effects produced upon the human organism by alcohol.

While we are not willing to admit Dr. Harris's statement that alcohol was the cause of crime, this quotation nevertheless shows to what a tremendous extent the criminal classes are addicted to alcoholism. The drug habit is found to be almost universal among them as well as the use of some form of tobacco.

The criminal finds another strong form of excitement in gambling. The love of cards is even more widely spread among them than the love of drink. Their stupidity and cunning are closely related. Mace, a former chief of Parisian *Police de Sûreté* remarks in spite of the cunning and tricks which are too gratuitously credited to thieves, their stupidity generally is scarcely credible; they nearly all resemble the ostrich who, when his head is hidden behind a leaf, thinks he is not seen because he cannot see.[1]

Untruthfulness is universal among criminals, due, perhaps, to the lack of moral sense. Their untruthfulness is exceeded by their vanity only. Their great ambition is to " die game." Their intelligence is of a low order and their language is " slang." We are told the French criminal possesses seventy-two terms for expressing the act of drinking and thirty-six for money. They have an elaborate system of signs and pictures and, according to Lombroso, a style of writing of their own.

Remorseless and cruel, the criminal seldom regrets his conduct. Out of more than 400 murderers known to Bruce Thompson only three expressed remorse. The moral insensibility of the instinctive criminal is the cause of his cruelty, which he frequently displays in his childhood. Rossi found in ten of his 100 criminals an exaggerated and precocious cruelty; one of them as a child used to take young birds, pull out their feathers, and roast them alive.[2]

Speaking of the immoral and indecent practices so common among criminals, Ellis says, " Such practices grow up chiefly as a means of excitement and diversion in vacuous lives. Love in its highest forms seems to be extremely rare. The love even when strong remains rather brutal. When a man was asked if he really loved the woman for whose sake he had murdered her husband, he replied, " Oh! You should have seen her naked." [3]

Yet more interesting than resort to external stimuli and more significant of emotional instability are the spontaneous outbursts of excitement among criminals which Dostoieffsky has studied. After living a quiet and peaceful life for several years prisoners frequently become un-

[1] Ellis, *The Criminal*, p. 155.

[2] *Op. cit.*, p. 147.   [3] *Op. cit.*, p. 170.

controllable and stop at no crime. It is a sort of desire " to affirm the degraded ego," the personality " born out of its time."

According to Ellis, a greater tendency to recidivism among women has been noted, especially in England, where it is rapidly increasing. In spite of this fact the proportion of women prisoners in the United States is very low, there being about one woman to every twelve men in custody in 1890. An interesting hypothesis is advanced in explanation of this fact by Marro who has suggested that sexual selection has exerted a marked influence in diminishing the criminality of woman. Masculine, unsexed and ugly, abnormal women—that is, the women most strongly marked with the signs of degeneration—would be to a large extent passed by in the choice of a mate. Others have suggested that the female criminality is kept down by woman's position in the home and by the greater oversight and protection of growing girls. This theory is borne out by the fact that the number of offenses committed by women has risen in keeping with the entrance of women into industrial occupations. However, Marro's theory must go far to explain the case. The female offender is shortlived and often degenerate, two very powerful factors in keeping her progeny down to a minimum.

Such is the rather gruesome description of our criminal, better of our criminal class. Probably Lombroso's criminal type never lived, and if he did, we could not be sure he would be criminal, but the fact is growing daily more certain that the criminal is a being apart. Marked off from normal society by his characteristics as well as by his deeds, he is bound more and more closely to his kind by the same twofold bond. Born, for the most part, of criminal or degenerate parents, the criminal early gives himself up to unknown forces within him. Growing up in an atmosphere of crime, he is an apt pupil of his veteran masters with whom he loves to associate. Unrestrained by moral sentiment within or without and early seized and handled in a barbarous manner by the officers of the social system which he so little understands and of which he is not a part, he soon becomes a hopeless derelict upon a boundless sea, driven and tossed by the tempests and tides of fate.

CHAPTER II

The Criminal Classes

THUS far we have spoken of the criminal class. This includes all persons who commit crime. A more particular investigation reveals numerous subdivisions in the group which have been differently classified by different writers. We find certain individuals committing certain crimes, another group committing other crimes; and Lombroso and others even go so far as to assert that there are physical anomalies characteristic of each group. As early as 1880 Ferri divided the entire body of criminals into five categories which he described as criminal madmen, born criminals, criminals by contracted habits, occasional criminals, and criminals of passion.[1] To this group Henderson suggests adding a class called professional criminals and Proal would include the political criminal. Henderson omits the group given by Ferri as criminal madmen.[2] Drähms reduces Ferri's five classes to three without mentioning the professional criminal. These he gives as the instinctive criminal, the habitual criminal, and the single offender. Working on the basis which he uses in eliminating the several other categories, one might go still further and present only one class including all criminals, which plan would defeat its own ends. Hence as a matter of convenience for the purposes of this volume we make the arbitrary division given on the next page.

[1] *Criminal Sociology,* p. 24.

[2] *Defectives, Dependents and Delinquents,* pp. 219 *et seq.*

463]

Fig. 1.

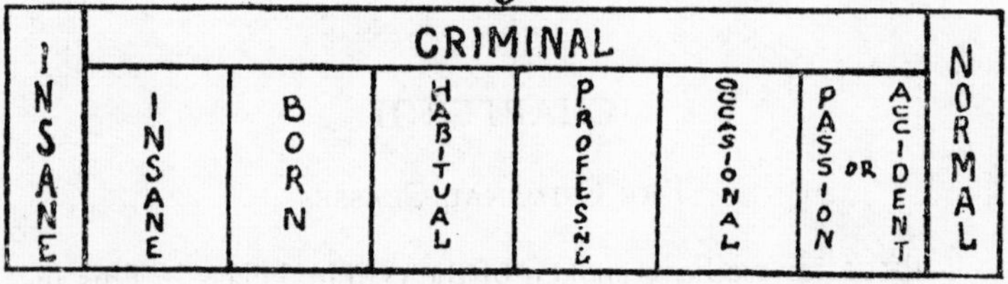

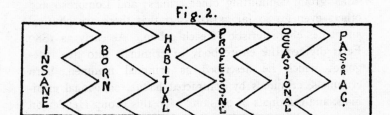

That these groups are not distinct from one another but
that they shade imperceptibly into each other is probably
better shown by figure two.

Fig. 2.

Even here confusion may arise from the order in which
the classes are placed, which is the logical order for a large
majority of the cases but which cannot be assumed for the
whole criminal group. For instance, the occasional criminal may be, and, we think, is a born criminal or a criminal
because of inherited physical or mental conditions; again,
the professional criminal may be associated with the born,
habitual, or occasional group. Hence to give a clearer idea
of the indefinite shading of the classes one into another we
have given the following.

Fig. 3.

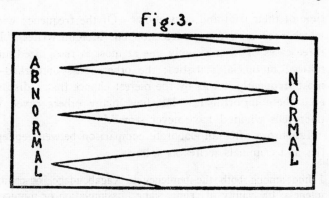

The insane criminal. In stating his reason for discarding Ferri's term " criminal madmen," Drähms asserts that the term means nothing. Either a man is a criminal or he is a madman. If he is a madman he cannot be a criminal.[1] Considered in the light of our definition of crime a man can be and frequently is both a madman and a criminal. The usual objection repeated by M. Joly which holds the term criminal madness to be self-contradictory, since a madman is not morally responsible and therefore cannot be a criminal, is not conclusive. We maintain that responsibility to society, the only responsibility common to all criminals, exists also for the criminal of unsound mind.[2] Allison tells us that the number of life convicts who are insane is about 25% of the total number of life men in New York and there is about the same proportion in Massachusetts and Broadmoor, Eng., showing that a great many life men either become insane while undergoing imprisonment or have committed their crimes through insanity which was not recognized at the

---

[1] *The Criminal,* p. 53.

[2] Ferri, *Criminal Sociology,* p. 26.

time of their trial and conviction.[1]   Of the frequency with
which such cases escape detection Dr. McKim writes, " In
three cases of insanity only one at most is recognized and
noticed in official statistics; the others pass unmarked—
most frequently it was by the merest chance that I discovered these unfortunates—but how many others raved in
their cells whom I have never seen." [2]

Lombroso after an elaborate comparison between epileptics and criminals writes as follows:

I find among both the tendency to vagabondage, obscenity,
idleness, the vanity of crime, slang, dissimulation or mimicry,
absence of character, instantaneous irritability, intermittence
in sentiments and intelligence, cowardice; both backward in
the personal equation relative to people normally constituted,
with tendency to contradict themselves and exaggerate everything.   In both morbid irritability, bad character ; both deluded
and suspicious.

The forms of the mania of these criminals are numerous
and varied.   It may be homicidal, suicidal, sexual, anti-
social, and often religious.   Frequently it takes the form
of a mania for burning things.   A case recently came to my
knowledge of continuous fires of incendiary origin, nearly
all the buildings being barns in the same locality.   Finally
the criminality was detected in a young man of normal
intelligence and good standing, well known as a clerk in
the community where the crimes had been committed.
Such persons are afflicted with a form of malady known
as paranoia by which is meant a condition of mind characterized by the presence of fixed delusions with, perhaps,
halucinations but without other evidence of insanity.   Of

[1] *Care and Custody of the Insane.*
[2] *Heredity and Human Progress,* p. 27.

such persons Dr. McKim writes, " Prone, through the nature of their disease, they readily accept the idea that society is an oppressor and possessed of an irresistible purpose they proceed to wreak a disastrous vengeance." In many persons this exists in a vague form which Maudsley describes as an insane temperament. At the conclusion of this description he writes:

All our present concern is to recognize distinctly that there is such a temperament, which, though by no means abolishing an individual's responsibility, must be taken into account when deeds of violence are done which seem to mark the outbreak of actual mental derangement. Unwarrantable as it may appear to assume a crime to be evidence of insanity when there have not been any previous symptoms to indicate disease, it is still possible that a crime may mark the period when an insane tendency has passed into actual insanity—when the weak organ has given away under the strain put upon it.[1]

In the same work Maudsley quotes Hoffbauer on the responsibility of persons committing crime under such conditions and comments as follows: Hoffbauer proposed that in order to answer the question of responsibility in regard to the acts of insane persons " the dominant impression in which their delusion consists should be regarded not as an error but as a truth; in other words, their actions ought to be considered as if they had been committed under the circumstances under which the individual believed himself to act." [2] If the imaginary circumstances make no change as to the imputability of the crime, then they ought to have no effect on the case under consideration; if they lessen or destroy culpability they ought to have that effect in a sup-

[1] Maudsley, *Responsibility in Mental Disease*, p. 57.
[2] *Op. cit.*, p. 209.

posed instance. The man is to be assumed to have a dual being—a sane and an insane personality; and accordingly as he acts in the former or the latter capacity is he to be condemned as a criminal or acquitted as a mad man. If Mr. Maudsley would substitute the word committed for acquitted we would accept his comment without remark other than to say that the responsibility of the criminal to society is the same in either of the above cases. With Ferri we maintain that responsibility to society, the only responsibility common to all criminals, exists also for the criminal of unsound mind.

In this group must be included all the intermediary types between madness and a rational condition, who remain in what Maudsley calls the " middle zone." Individuals of this group mingle freely and unfeared with society today and become the horrible criminals of tomorrow. Here stands the *fou* of Tarde " who is isolated, a stranger to all and a stranger to himself . . . by nature unsocial as well as irresponsible, and the one, perhaps, on account of the other; he is not supra-social in any manner like the genius, he is only extra-social." [1] Capable of perpetrating any crime which may be conceived in his idiot brain, he looms above our social life, an ever-present menace to our peace and happiness.

The born criminal. Much that has been said of the insane criminal applies equally to the born criminal. Some have gone so far as to assert that all criminality is due to a species of insanity. If by this term one means merely a departure from the normal we have no objection to its use. Green assumes that criminality is the result of a diseased condition of the criminal which is but stating the same thing in new terms. [2] Either term is applicable to the born crim-

[1] *Criminalité comparée*, p. 26.   [2] *Crime.*

inal. To say that a man is insane assumes that he is not
functioning normally mentally. To assert that he is born
in this condition is to assert that his normal condition is
an insane one, which is an absurdity. A born criminal,
therefore, is neither insane nor diseased in the sense in
which these terms have been used. His normal condition
is abnormal only as compared to the ordinary individual,
hence his conduct is not abnormal but the natural result
of his normal condition. In other words he is born to
crime. It is his natural function.

This group presents the largest number of physical and
mental criminal characteristics. The born criminal is cruel
and remorseless and usually given to serious or violent
crimes, although many petty offenders are of this group.
Born or instinctive criminals, writes Ferri,

are those who most frequently present the organic and psychological characteristics established by criminal anthropology.
These are either savage or brutal men, or crafty or idle, who
draw no distinction between homicide, robbery, and other
kinds of crime and honest industry. " They are criminals just
as others are good working men," says Frégier; and as
Romagnosi puts it, " actual punishment affects them less than
the menace of punishment or does not affect them at all, since
they regard imprisonment as a natural risk of their occupation,
as masons regard the fall of a roof or as miners regard fire-
damp." They do not suffer in prison. They are like a painter
in his studio dreaming of his next masterpiece. They are on
good terms with their gaolers and know how to make themselves useful.[1]

The hopelessness of trying to reform such persons is readily apparent. Some are known to have been incarcerated
as many as 200 times, showing their utter incapacity to lead

[1] *Op. cit.*, p. 28.

any other kind of existence. According to Ferri, there are very few cases in which a man or a woman who has turned thief ceases to be one. Whatever the reason may be, as a matter of fact a thief is rarely or never reformed. When you can turn an old thief into an honest worker, you can turn an old fox into a house dog.[1]

The habitual criminal. The habitual criminal differs from the born criminal, not that he is not born to crime— we believe he is—, but in that he is capable of something else, at least in one period in his life. The born criminal never is. It is merely a matter of degree. The habitual offender, born with a strong tendency to crime, with very feeble powers to resist his natural inclination, differs from the born criminal in that he is at first capable of pursuing an honest livelihood, but under the promptings of his inherent nature and, perhaps, some particularly tempting opportunity to steal or revenge himself for some real or imagined injury, his feeble moral powers give way and he becomes a criminal. The ease with which he is able to escape detection or the lightness of his punishment, if caught, serves to encourage him in future malpractice. After a time of this yielding to his criminal nature his moral powers, exceedingly slight at first, become totally atrophied. Such persons are, as Bruce Thompson says, true moral imbeciles; their moral insensibility is such that in the presence of temptation they have no control over themselves; and among all the murderers he had known, amounting to nearly five hundred, only three could be ascertained to have any remorse.

After the first few offences, the habitual criminal seldom, if ever, makes any attempt, and perhaps has no ability, to lead any other life; and such he continues as long as lib-

[1] *Op. cit.,* p. 35.

erty and life are allowed to him. Men of this type are almost invariably degenerates, moral imbeciles, or insane, and the family trees of such individuals indicate clearly the causal relations which heredity bears to crime. They represent about ¼ to ⅓ of all offenders; and, together with the instinctive criminal element (about 10%) compose perhaps 40% of the total recalcitrant population.[1]

The habitual criminal, writes McKim, is not at all the kind of being of whom we think when we talk of and plan for the spread of liberty, equality, and fraternity; in his very essence he is unchangeably incompatible with such privileges and with all higher life. Through the selfishness of his motives and his feeble self-control he is a creature whom we cannot admit to co-operation with us, one whom we must ever mistrust and fear.[2]

With regard to anomalies he does not differ essentially from the born criminal. His characteristics show a remarkable tendency to appear in proportion to the enormity of his crime. Usually the nature of his offence remains the same. Modifications, however, frequently occur as, for instance, when the burglar passes over into the professional safe-blower.

The professional criminal. The distinction between the professional and the habitual criminal is not marked. Unlike the habitual criminal, the professional criminal is frequently of a high order of intelligence,—often a college graduate. His profession becomes an art in which he sometimes becomes a master. Unlike the habitual criminal who follows his impulses into crime at his earliest opportunity, the professional sometimes spends years in the preparation for a single great offence. According to Byrnes, plans of vaults, walls, passages, and the important par-

[1] Drähms, *The Criminal*, p. 194.   [2] McKim, *op. cit.*, p. 6.

ticulars of some large financial institutions have been in the possession of certain " gangs " of noted criminals for years, having been drawn up and "bequeathed" by experts long dead or serving life sentences in penitentiaries. Ordinarily the professional criminal makes his operations worth while. There is none of the aimlessness of the habitual criminal about him. His operations are always to obtain money or things of value easily transferable into money. Occasionally he commits murder but it is almost invariably to escape detection. He refrains from doing injury to persons or taking life, if possible, but when necessary to his security or escape, no crime or series of crimes is too heinous for him to commit.

During his long periods of inactivity he supports himself by gambling; not infrequently by carrying on a legitimate business—the latter, however, more frequently serves as a screen to cover preparations for some new enterprise. In some cases, he makes elaborate preparations for the disposal of his booty, while in others he is at the end of his resourcefulness the moment his plans are successfully carried out and the treasure is in his possession.

Many professionals make allowance for possible time spent in prison, making their " haul " of sufficient magnitude to furnish ample reward for the period of incarceration. On the other hand, some of the most noted and most successful ones invariably follow up a " killing " with a period of debauch which ends only with the exhaustion of their suddenly acquired fortunes and which not infrequently leads to their detection and arrest.

Sometimes the professional works alone, again as a part of a well-organized gang, but most frequently in company with one or two trusted " pals," as expert as himself in planning and perpetrating great crimes. His plunder varies in value from a nickel to a quarter of a million dollars, in accordance with the nature of his profession. The gains of pick-pockets, sneak-thieves, and shop-lifters are usually small. The large army of burglars, robbers, lock-pickers, safe-crackers, confidence men, " green goods " men, swindlers, and forgers uniformly plans for large " hauls." As would be expected, the most difficult kinds of crime are undertaken only when the prospect of plunder is greatest. When some great scheme has been put through with slight results, it is invariably because the perpetrator has made some miscalculation or some detail has been overlooked in the study of the situation beforehand. Some of the most noted professionals have been known to have secured as a sum of their enterprises amounts of money approaching the million mark.

Physically, the professional criminal differs little from the habitual criminal. Quite frequently an occasional criminal at first, he learns to make criminality worth while. This knowledge is acquired at the total expense of, or in the entire absence of the moral sense. Bound by no social tie, he is a true parasite. He presents no menace to life unless interfered with in his occupation, but no human device has yet been perfected to secure our worldly goods against him. Very rarely has he been known to return to an honest life after " graduation " in his chosen activity.

The occasional criminal. This type forms a considerable portion of the criminal population and, as a class, is well defined. The occasional criminal is essentially a born criminal, but differs from the group thus designated, largely in the matter of degree of criminality. While the normal function of our born criminal is crime *at all times,* the occasional criminal yields to his inherent tendencies *intermittently,* sometimes periodically.

Different efforts have been made, especially by Lombroso and Ferri, to distinguish between the occasional criminal and the criminal born. The latter seeks to differentiate them on the basis of their activity, the other largely on the basis of physical characteristics. Drähms refuses to make any distinction between the occasional criminal and the habitual offender. Lombroso sub-divides the occasional group into " pseudo-criminals," *i. e.,* those who are normal beings and who commit involuntary offenses, or offenses which do not spring from perversity, and do not hurt society, although punishable by law; and " criminaloids," who commit ordinary offenses, but differ from born criminals both in their activity and physical characteristics. The latter group we consider to be true occasional criminals; the former we hardly consider criminals in the real sense. That Lombroso did not either, is indicated by his designation of them as " false " criminals, *i. e.,* not really criminals. However, since they are malefactors and therefore demand consideration, we have placed them in our group of criminals by passion or accident.

Occasional criminals are known to almost every community. Frequently their crime is of a petty nature and does not bring about their incarceration for any considerable length of time. In many the inner force which seems to simmer for long periods before boiling over, spends itself in several days of debauch or a drunken " spree," after which outburst the individual returns to his normal state and remains thus until again overpowered by his ever-present enemy. In some this outburst takes the form of crime, either petty or serious according to the nature of the conditions prevailing at the time of the explosion. Of these Maudsley says, " If they did not commit crime they would go mad, and they do not go mad because they are criminals." The close relation between this group and the insane criminal is here evident.

The following passage from Lombroso shows the degree of difference between the occasional and the born criminal.

Occasional criminals or criminaloids have shown me the weakened but still very visible characteristics of criminals born. Sensibility is less obtuse, reflexes are less irregular, anomalies are less frequent especially in the skull. Some abnormal characteristics, however, appear, as, hair blacker among domestic thieves and left-handedness among common thieves. Great impulsiveness is found among all, and, what one least expects, great precocity.[1]

The born criminal as well as the habitual criminal differs according to Ferri, from the occasional criminal because the first is pushed to crime by an interior force, acquired or innate, from which comes a strange pleasure that he tastes in doing evil; while the latter, when a exterior force impells him, is not held in honesty by a sufficient repugnance.

Unlike the criminals of the groups already described, the occasional criminal frequently possesses a keen sense of remorse, which, however, is not operative during the period of criminality. Frequently after his aberrations his self-loathing amounts almost to melancholia. Here, for the first time, environment plays an important part in the nature of the crime committed.

The occasional criminal is not always anti-social. On the contrary, between the outbursts of his criminal personality, he is frequently a useful citizen. He rarely ever succeeds in escaping from his malady and the law offers no assistance. Fear of punishment and moral restraint part company with him the moment his dread second-self assumes control of his being.

[1] *L'Anthropologie criminelle*, p. 92.

The menace to a community of a criminal of this type is vastly underestimated. On account of his moral condition, normally, and the petty nature of his crime, he is not considered dangerous by his fellow citizens. Yet no one knows at what minute the petty crimes may be followed by a tragedy, made more heinous because of the exceptional opportunity offered for its perpetration.

The criminal by passion or accident. The heading of this section goes far to describe the group thus characterized. The only grave question raised by this classification is in regard to the criminality of this group. Is the criminal by passion or accident a true criminal? So slight are the physical indications of criminality found in him that one must hesitate to identify him as such upon this ground. But, in the sense that his conduct has endangered or injured the social well-being of his group, he is. For this reason he must be considered in this work. Of this type Dr. Drähms writes:

This class lies, properly speaking, outside the pale of true criminalism, while indubitably sharing in the common reprobation affixed by law and custom. Culpable by an isolated offence, possibly as the outcome of a train of antecedent circumstances and secondary causes that received their initiative from a state of affairs for which society itself is largely to blame, he has never, in the past, doubtless will not again in the future so challenge public sentiment and violate the letter of the law as to pillory him upon its bosses because of transgressional shortcomings.

The accidental nature of his offenses is often manifest. On account of this, his criminality covers a wide range. There are no crimes that can be said to be characteristic unless one should use the broad term " crimes of violence " especially in regard to those committed in a moment of

passion. To what extent crime may be accidental is well
shown by the following extract from a pamphlet by Mc-
Donald : " The study of the criminal can also be the study of
the normal man; for most criminals are so by occasion or
accident and differ in no respect from other men. Thus an
individual, becoming excited in discussion, or under the influence of liquor, or on account of an insult, may, on the
spur of the moment, strike the offender with the nearest
object in reach; if it is a hammer, he is a criminal; if it is
a book, he is not." [1]

Again, the activity which is not criminal in one locality
may occur by chance in a locality where it is prohibited by
law. The unsuspecting person becomes a criminal in this
case by the mere accident of location at the moment of his
activity. In this group we place Lombroso's " pseudo-
criminal " who is not in any sense anti-social. Frequently
his crime is that of omission, and most frequently one of
ignorance.

The criminal of passion, says Ferri, is one who is strong
enough to resist ordinary temptations, to which the occasional criminal would yield, but who does not resist psychological storms of sometimes irresistible power.

Often the most desperate crimes are perpetrated by the
criminal of passion from a sense of duty so high as, in his
estimation, to rise superior to the law. Such persons glory
in their punishment and look upon themselves as martyrs to
their higher code. Again there is the person who is so
completely carried away by his feelings as to lose control
of himself for the time being. Jealousy, hatred, desire for
revenge, and insults frequently rouse persons to crime
who are subject to what is commonly known as " high
temper," " fits of passion," etc. Others commit crime as

[1] *Criminology.*

the result of outraged justice or decency.   Continuous newspaper references to the " unwritten law " testify to the frequency of this form of crime.   These persons constitute a
large part of the group which Drähms designates as the
" single offender," for the reason that they are seldom
recidivists.

Among other symptoms of the criminal of passion, says
Ferri, there is also the precise motive which leads to a
crime complete in itself, and never as a means of attaining
another criminal purpose.   These offenders immediately
acknowledge their crime, with a remorse frequently so keen
that they instantly commit, or attempt to commit, suicide.

The astonishing frequence of what is designated by the
newspapers as " double crime " is the result of a high proportion of these " high-tempered " individuals in our population.   The first crime is most frequently the work of a
criminal by passion, the second is his self-destruction or attempted self-destruction on account of remorse.   Outraged
justice or decency frequently leads the most virtuous into
crime.   When convicted they are always repentant and are
seldom corrupted by prison life.   In them we very rarely
observe the physical and mental anomalies characteristic
of criminals.

In the case of criminals of this group we feel that no so-
called " cure " is necessary.   They are not immoral and
punishment in most cases is disastrous and a gross injustice.
These persons are unfortunate in possessing an insufficient
amount of self-control to resist stimuli which come upon
them from within and without.

Much has already been said of the defective moral sense
or so-called moral blindness in criminals.   This occurs in
varying degrees in the various groups.   It consists of total
or partial absence of appreciation of moral restraint; or of

what Sutherland calls the moral instinct.[1] This power, which in the normal man keeps him from crime, is partially or wholly lacking in the criminal. Speaking of this faculty Maudsley says: " Its sanction is given to such actions as are conducive to the well-being and progress of the race, and its prohibitions to such as would, if freely indulged in, lead to the degeneration if not the extinction of mankind; in other words, when it is in healthy functional action, its functions, like that of any other part of the body are conducive to the well-being of the organism; when it is not exercised it decays, and so leads to individual degeneration and, through individuals, to degeneracy of race."

Ferri thinks occasional crime is due especially to improvidence, while inborn and habitual crime are due to moral insensibility. In the born criminal it is, above all, the lack or the weakness of the moral sense which prevents him from understanding crime, whereas in the occasional criminal the moral sense is almost normal, but his inability to realize beforehand the consequences of his act causes him to yield to external influences.

[1] *The Origin and Development of the Moral Sentiments.*

CHAPTER III

The Formula of Crime

We are now ready to assert what we have already suggested in answer to our initial question, given your criminal, *why is he a criminal?*

An incident occurs in a group of individuals which stirs each one of them to action. While the stimulus is the same for each, no two respond to it in exactly the same manner. Necessarily, each responds as a result of the influence of the stimulus upon his own peculiar self. He could not do otherwise. Hence the nature of each individual response depends upon the nature of each individual and his entire activity is the expression of his individuality.

So long as each individual acts in a manner tolerable to his group he is classed as normal, *i. e.,* not differing materially from his fellows. When the activity is or becomes intolerable to his associates he is abnormal, *i. e.,* his conduct differs from that of his fellows to such an extent as to be insufferable. When his abnormality is such that his activity is a menace to his group, precautionary measures are necessary for the protection of society against him. He is a criminal because of his abnormality and crime is his natural function. In other words, *crime is the normal function of an abnormal man.* It is the very expression of his being, his personality. Therefore the criminal is a criminal because he is so constituted that the natural expression of his self, his personality, in response to stimuli is crime. We

46

believe this conclusion to be borne out by the preceding chapters which testify to the physical, mental, and moral abnormality of the " criminal man " The combination of stimuli and the criminal personality result in crime just as naturally as H_2O=Water. But the figures differ in one respect. The chemical formula is invariable, the proportions must be constant; but the criminal formula permits of variation in the constituent parts, the result remaining the same. For the sake of clearness, let us state the proposition thus: Criminal personality, stimuli=Crime. Or C-P, S=Crime. In Chemistry there must be two parts of Hydrogen to one part of Oxygen to produce water. In criminology the result is the same as long as the sum of the constituent parts amounts to crime; C-P4, S4=Crime(8) or C-P2, S6=Crime(8). In this manner proportionate tables can be constructed for the various classes of criminals which will make an evident distinction between them, for instance, why the born criminal commits crime continually and why the criminal by passion only once. In the first three groups of our classification, and, perhaps, the fourth, the amount or nature of the stimuli is of very little importance.

Fig. 4.

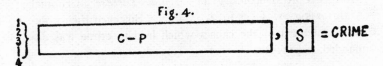

So predominant is the criminal nature in these cases that the activity is criminal almost regardless of what the stimuli may be.

Fig.5.

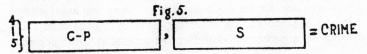

In the fifth group and perhaps a part of the fourth, the criminal personality is such that under a great many circumstances the response to stimuli is not of a criminal nature; only when the stimulus is of considerable force does the personality react in a criminal manner.

Fig. 6.

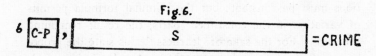

In group six the personality is so slightly criminal that under practically all circumstances its reaction is normal conduct. Only when the force of circumstances is practically overwhelming does the personality respond in a criminal manner; but the response is, nevertheless, a natural result of the interaction of the self and its environment.

The latter part of our problem is more difficult of solution. Given your criminal; from what source does he arise? The long-accepted theory of a depraved nature no longer satisfies the scientific inquirer. Thirty years ago, scholars were just beginning to seek for a more satisfactory explanation of criminality and its origin. When Maudsley wrote his *Responsibility in Mental Diseases* Criminal Anthropology was yet in its infancy. But even then a definite statement of the causes which lead to crime was demanded. He wrote:

Not until comparatively recently has much attention been given to the way in which criminals are produced. It was with them much as it was the lunatics; to say of the former that they were wicked, and of the latter that they were mad, was thought to render any further explanation unnecessary and any further inquiry superfluous. It is certain, however, that lunatics and criminals are as much manufactured articles as steam engines and calico-printing machines, only the processes of the organic manufacture are so complex that we are not able to follow them. They are neither accidents nor anomalies, but come by law and testify to causality; and it is the business of science to find out what the causes are and by what laws they work. There is nothing accidental, nothing supernatural, in the impulse to do wrong or in the impulse to do right; both come by inheritance or by education; and science can no more rest content with the explanation which attributes one to the grace of Heaven and the other to the malice of the Devil, than it could rest content with the explanation of insanity as a possession by the Devil.[1]

In answer to such statements as these, various theories have been put forth to explain the condition of our criminal man. That the criminal is a product of society we have already explained. So definitely may he be said to be the result of social and environmental forces acting with physiological forces, that Ferri has been able to maintain his theory of Criminal Saturation. " Just as in a given body of water at a given temperature, we find a solution of a fixed quantity of any chemical substance, not an atom more or less, so in a given social environment, in certain defined physical conditions of the individual, we find the commission of a fixed number of crimes." [2]   The very statement of our formula necessitates a two-fold investigation of the causes or sources of crime. The personality which reacts upon stimuli in a criminal manner requires an anthropological or biological investigation; the stimuli which cause such actions on the part of the criminal personality necessitate sociological study. Any study based upon either of these alone is not complete, no matter how enlightening. For a comprehensive explanation of the presence and condition of our

[1] p. 28.   [2] *Criminal Sociology,* p. 76.

criminal, both must be taken into consideration.   Probably
the best example of such a study is Ferri's *Criminal Sociology.*

The theory of atavism—the reappearance of old types
—was early set forth by Lombroso.   Basing his conclusions
upon the appearance in cadavers of criminals of numerous
abnormalities peculiar to the lower savages and animals,
especially the anthropoid apes, he affirmed that the criminal was a man born out of his time—in a wrong age so to
speak.   Thus Hack Tuke, in his book, *Case of Congenital Moral Defect,* describing a typical case of moral imbecility, remarks: " Such a man as this is a reversion to an
old-type savage, and is born by accident in the wrong century.   He would have had sufficient scope for his blood-thirsty propensities, and been in harmony with his environment in a barbaric age or at the present day in certain parts
of Africa."

Later, however, Lombroso discovered numerous anomalies in criminals which are not possessed by savages or animals, or at least, which are not characteristic of them.
This led him to reject his atavistic theory in part in favor
of one of degeneracy.   The parts of this two-fold theory,
however, are not antagonistic; each accounts for a large
number of criminals.

Another theory which accounts for large numbers of
criminals is the theory of " arrested development " as set
forth by Ellis in *The Criminal.*   This theory is based
on the biological hypothesis that the individual, from the
moment of his conception to maturity, passes through all
the stages of the evolution of his kind.   For some reason or
other, in the case of the criminal, this developmental process is checked at a point which leaves the individual a
savage, fitted for a strenuous life, in the midst of a society
which has centuries before outgrown, on the whole, all

need for his kind. Again, it is asserted, the criminal is
an individual who, to an extent, remains a child his life long
—a child of larger growth and of greater capacity for evil.

Maudsley has made a valuable contribution to the study
of the criminal by showing that crime is frequently due to
the approach of insanity, and, in many cases, it marks the
point of departure from a normal to an abnormal state, a
step in the process of mind degeneration. He accounts for
this on the ground of moral perversion which, he asserts,
is characteristic of the approach of insanity. " The last acquired faculty in the progress of human evolution is the
first to suffer when disease invades the mental organiza-
tion." In addition to this loss of the moral sense it is observed that, in extreme cases, the modest man becomes
presumptuous and exacting, the chaste man lewd and obscene, the honest man a thief, and the truthful man an
unblushing liar. Short of this, however, there in an ob-
servable impairment of the finer moral feelings—a something different which his friends do not fail to feel, although
they can not always describe it.

No doubt each of the foregoing explanations accounts
in a way for a large number of criminals: but as yet no
theory has been advanced which adequately accounts for
criminality as a whole. The theory of atavism may be true
in that the criminal is a man born out of his generation.
but as a statement of fact it does not give a reason for the
fact. Granted that the criminal is the reappearance of an
old type, why does he appear? The same thing may be said
of degeneration. Why has the process of degeneration appeared in his particular case? Under given circumstances.
why does one individual or stock degenerate and not another? The following theory is set forth as an effort to
answer these questions. It is presented tentatively because
the author has not had opportunity to substantiate it, if

this were indeed possible. If in the future it may be substantiated, its presentation will be justified; if the demonstration of its fallaciousness should suggest to some future investigator a more plausible explanation, it will have accomplished, in part, the end desired by the writer in setting it forth.

This theory is based upon the same biological assumption as that of atavism, namely, that numerous life germs or cells, or infinitesimal somethings which subsequently enter into the composition of the germ cells, are transmitted through individuals for numerous generations. To these are added and with them transmitted new and more highly developed characters as the stock receives beneficient infusions of blood from advantageous crossings. But because of conditions under which the types bearing the older characteristics came into being, they are better fitted to survive and appear under conditions which are fatal to either the existance or the appearance of the newer or more highly developed ones. Thus it happens that under disturbed or unfavorable conditions the older types appear because of their fitness to do so. Thus the moral sense, which is perhaps the latest acquisition of the race, is not found in the criminal or in a very low form only. The astonishing absence of this sense is shown by the examination of 8828 inmates of Elmira Reformatory which resulted in the following conclusions:

Susceptibility to moral impressions (*estimated*)

Positively none	3203 or	36.3 per cent
Possibly some	3432 or	38.9 per cent
Ordinarily susceptible	1814 or	20.5 per cent
Specially susceptible	379 or	4.3 per cent

Moral sense (even such as show under examination either filial affection, sense of shame, or personal loss)

Absolutely none .... 2618 or 29.7 per cent
Possibly some .... 3687 or 41.8 per cent
Ordinarily sensitive .... 2022 or 22.9 per cent
Specially sensitive .... 501 or 5.6 per cent

It is a fact patent to gardeners and persons who keep and breed fancy stock of any kind that under the most favorable circumstances only do highly-developed animals or varieties produce progeny equal to themselves in excellence and very rarely superior. Left to themselves the stock and variety would rapidly deteriorate according to our standards of excellence to stocks and varieties which would be suited to the conditions under which they originated. It is also well known that great individuals in history have rarely left descendants who achieved greatness, while many of them left no progeny at all.

Groups of ever so heterogeneous persons forced to live perpetually in a given environment, tend to approach a type best suited to exist under the existing conditions. If the conditions demand a savage the savage ultimately appears. Atavism, then, is the appearance of an old type because that type was the only one or the best one fitted to appear under the circumstances. Degeneration occurs as the result of the appearance of a certain type susceptible to disintegration, or of a type developed under unfavorable influences.

In the field of degeneration, prenatal influences play an important part. Here the embryo may be subjected to conditions which will prohibit the possibility of it in turn producing a normal progeny or any at all. Thus we revert again to our fundamental explanation. Arrested development may account for that person who was subjected to demoralizing prenatal influences; but may it not be possible, also, that the so-called victim of arrested development may be only an old type developed to its fullest capacity, which has appeared as a result of the peculiar conditions under which it was conceived?

The intense struggle for existence cannot fail to leave its debris in the wake of progress, as, perhaps, do great political and religious agitations. The influence of war is marked. According to Keurella, a rapid increase of the number of youthful criminals in Germany has been shown since 1887. He thinks this due, in part, to the shattering of nerves and general weakness in fathers—and we may reasonably add the anxiety of mothers—induced by the bloody wars of 1870, and in part to the influence of the feeble men who remained at home and married while the strong and manly were at the seat of war. With this accords the fact given by Marro that in France the recruits of 1833 and 1834 born in 1812-13 (war years), were the feeblest of the century. Akin to these observations is the fact that, out of 92 children born in Paris during the great siege of 1870-1, 64 had mental or physical anomalies and the remaining 28 were weakly, 81 were intellectually defective and 8 showed moral or emotional insanity. These defective children were popularly known as *enfants du siège.*[1]

With the numerous additional influences under which these types tend to appear we are not prepared to deal further than to classify them under three heads, namely, pre-conceptual or operating at the moment of conception, pre-natal, and post-natal; the last two, of course, not operative until the next generation when they properly become pre-conceptual. Disparity in the ages of parents has been noted as an additional cause and most remarkable is the abnormally large proportion of criminals with parents be-

---

[1] McKim, *Heredity and Human Progress*, p. 106.

longing to the period of decadence. According to Ellis it
is most marked among the murderers, 52.9 per cent of
whose fathers had passed the period of maturity; but it is
very large, also, exceeding the insane, among those convicted
of assault and wounding and among sharpers. Dr. Lang-
don Down finds that in 23 per cent of the cases he had
studied there had been a disparity of age of more than ten
years at the birth of the idiot child, the father in nearly
every case being the older, and that in many cases this disparity has reached more than 25 years. Among other
causes that may be enumerated are drunkenness and debauchery, together with all influences which tend to lower
vitality and contaminate the blood. That many criminals
are born of criminals testifies to the fact that in them criminal types predominate. Such notable instances of criminal
families as the Jukes lead one to believe them, in many instances, incapable of producing normal offspring except
by an infusion of new blood; and even this loses its beneficent effects in the second generation.

CHAPTER IV

PUNISHMENT

THE idea of punishment is a complex one and it is not our intention to go into detailed or scientific discussion of its origin or history. A very brief summary of these topics will suffice for the purpose of this work. The idea of punishment is so mixed with instinct and barbarous vengeance that it is difficult to define it without being arbitrary. According to a generally-accepted theory, it has its origin in the instinct of self-defense which broadens into social defense, as, for example, when a herd of elephants drive out a criminal or so-called bad elephant from among them.

To the idea of punishment personal vengeance has contributed much. In many cases it takes the form of social vengeance. As a result of this many of the brutal forms of barbarism survived far over into our present civilization, although a great deal of the cruelty was probably a result of an effort on the part of society to intimidate the offender and deter others. In medieval times, whipping, branding, mutilation and dismemberment, and disgraceful public exposure were the common physical punishments short of death. In England those who refused to plead were, until 1772, pressed, *i. e.,* heavy weights were placed on their prostrate bodies till they gave in or died. Mutilations were sometimes inflicted with great cruelty. Ears were nailed to the pillory so that the movement of the body tore them off. William Pryne lost his ears by sentence of the Star Chamber for seditious publications. The Earl of Dorset, in pro-

nouncing sentence, expressed his personal opinion that he
should be loth that he should escape with his ears. " Therefore I would have him branded in the forehead, slit in the
nose, and his ears cropt too." Three years later Pryne lost
the remainder of his ears, and was branded S. L.—seditious
libeler—on both cheeks. Women were whipped besides
being put in the pillory. Usually women were flogged in
private, but not always, even up till the end of the 18th century; the men in public, sometimes in the gates of the
market place of the town, or for 100 or 200 yards through
the streets.[1] As late as the 19th century a prominent English writer on criminal law expressed himself as follows:
" I think it highly desirable that criminals should be hated,
that punishment inflicted upon them should be so contrived
as to give expression to that hatred, and to justify it so far
as the public provision of means for expressing and gratifying a healthy natural sentiment can justify and encourage it." [2]
The present-day purpose of punishment was long ago
expressed by Beccaria, whose views were far in advance of
his time. " The end of punishment, therefore, is no other
than to prevent the criminal from doing further injury to
society, and to prevent others from committing the like
offense. Such punishments, therefore, and such a mode of
inflicting them ought to be chosen as will make the strongest and most lasting impression on the minds of others,
with the least torment to the body of the criminal."[3] Even
modern law in divers countries allots punishment according
to the degrees of free-will with which the criminal acts or
more or less severely according as the crime was premedi-

[1] DuCane, *The Punishment and Prevention of Crime.*
[2] Stephen.
[3] *Essay.*

tated or perpetrated with criminal intent. Against such and like conditions Ellis cries out: " our law is still in so semi-barbaric a condition that the grave interests of society and of the individual are made to hinge on a problem which often must be insoluble." For instance . . . " it cannot make the slightest difference whether the criminal is sane or insane. Sane or insane he is still noxious to society, and society must be protected from him. Sane or insane it is still our duty and our interest to treat him humanely, and to use all means in our power to render him capable of living a social life."

The purpose of punishment is twofold, namely, to protect society and reform the criminal. The interests of society are considered to be threefold—to protect itself from the present offender; to punish the offender, and to deter possible offenders. The interests of the individual are a reflex of the interests of society, *i. e.,* the reformation of the criminal himself and the salvation of one of the members of society. The accepted theory has been that this was to be accomplished by punishment and the conception of its deterrent influence is adequately expressed by Hume as follows: " All laws being founded on rewards and punishments, it is supposed, as a fundamental principle, that these motives have a regular and uniform influence on the mind, and both produce the good and prevent the evil actions." [1] Let us consider the foregoing propositions in the light of the conclusions arrived at in former chapters.

The Interests of Society. That society is the most progressive which permits the greatest amount of liberty to its members in the choice of commercial activity and in the pursuit of pleasures. In order to permit this liberty to the fullest extent the state must guarantee a reasonable amount

[1] *Inquiry Concerning Human Understanding,* sec. i, part ii.

of safety to the individual, including security for his vested
interests and the unmolested enjoyment of the fruits of
his labors.   Any activity which proves a menace to this
safety is, therefore, a menace to the society, and the perpetrator becomes a public enemy.   The enemy within is a
far greater menace than the enemy without, hence the paramount interest of society is that her internal enemies be sup-
pressed.   No matter what may be the cause or nature of
his enmity, society must protect itself against the criminal
at all hazards.   Neither insanity, moral insensibility, defective constitution, nor any other condition in the criminal
or conducive to the crime can relieve it of the obligation of
self-defense.

The earliest form of punishment was instinctive.   That
individual, either animal or savage, which was endowed
with the strongest instinct of self-defense was destined in
the long run to leave more and better endowed offspring
than his less fortunate brother.   As in all groups or aggre-
gations of living things that individual which departs too
much from the norm is marked for destruction, so, in a
group where the instinct of self-preservation was strong
in a majority of the members, the individual less endowed
with this instinct ultimately perished.   The stronger the
social bond becomes, the more the instinct of self-defense
passes over into the instinct of social defense.   Thus also,
the individual which is roused to a desire for vengeance
by pain becomes the norm of the group and personal vengeance passes over into social vengeance, the only form of
punishment to appear for a long period of time.

Thus we find the rudimentary form of punishment among
animals; it exists in a little higher state among savages,
and the crude, instinctive social defense survives to-day in
the highest civilizations, as manifested by the frequent riots,
mobs and lynchings occurring among us.

For this reason, as one would suspect, the earliest forms
of crime punished were those which were a menace to the
social group, for instance, incest, treason, and evil witch-
craft. These, in many groups, were the only forms of crime
to receive public atention. All three are highly dangerous
to society. All other offences were personal matters and
subject to vengeance. The growth of crime is due to the
passing over of acts from the field of personal injuries to
that of social injuries.

Tacitus tells us in the *Germania* that punishment among
the Germans varied with the crime; traitors and deserters
to the enemy were gibbeted alive on trees; cowards and
dastards, and men convicted of unnatural practices, were
suffocated in bogs under hurdles. Minor crimes (homicide,
adultery, theft, *etc.*) were punished on the same graduated
scale, *i. e.*, against public laws, publicly punished; against
natural laws, punished privately. The convicted were fined
according to the number of their horses or flocks, part of
which went to the king, the state, the injured person or his
relatives. Here we see minor offenses passing over into
social offenses. The personal nature of some of them is
still recognized by the allotment of a portion of the fine to
the injured party.

Punishment, then, is merely disguised or transformed
vengeance. The prevalent idea of blame attached to it is a
religious one, and first appears in punishment for sin. It
was naïvely supposed that the loss of one eye was made
good by the destruction of another.

Punishment never was truly moral. " True social punishment " (social vengeance), says Hall, " existed before
moral thought was possible, and it has generically nothing
whatever to do with the motives of the individual. It has
its roots deep in the necessity of self-defense, and is born
of instinctive social vengeance. It deals with acts and not

with motives, and its aim is the welfare of society, and not of the individual offender." [1]   True moral justice demands that the eye be restored or compensation given.   Punishment for the commission of a wrong act is not originally a social idea.   " The soul that sinneth it shall die," is a biological mandate as well as a spiritual one; but death is not as a punishment for sin, but as a·result of sin.

The idea of punishment must be eradicated from society's treatment of its criminals.   If the criminal is responsible for his crime, punishment satisfies neither society nor the injured party.   If he is not responsible, society injures not only the criminal but itself also by this barbarous procedure.

Punishment has long been retained as a preventive, a deterrent.   It is supposed that the sad fate of the condemned criminal will lead him to give up his unlawful career upon liberation in order to escape future discomforts; while the dread spectacle of his fate should restrain possible offenders by arousing in them fear of a like suffering.   On this point Ferri writes:

It is a natural law that forces cannot conflict or neutralize each other unless they are of the same kind.   The fall of a body cannot be retarded, changed in direction, or accelerated, save by a force homogeneous with that of gravity.   So punishment, as a psychological motive, can only oppose the psychological factors of crime, and indeed only the occasional and moderately energetic factors; for it is evident that it cannot, as a preliminary to its application, eliminate the organic hereditary factors which are revealed to us by criminal anthropology. [2]

There is a growing conviction that punishment does not

[1] *Crime and Social Progress*, p. 37.   [2] *Op. cit.*, p. 92.

deter. That this is true in part is noticed by Ross, who
says: " the reformatory idea rests upon the sound maxim
that only those should be punished who are amenable to
the dread of punishment. This would enjoin that all law-
breakers enjoying self-control and real power of choice
should be made to smart; but as to the mass of small-witted,
weak-willed, impulsive human ' screenings ' that collect in
prisons, our care should be to reform the reformable and to
hold fast the incurable the rest of their days." [1]

The insane, born and habitual criminals certainly are not
restrained by punishment; the professional deliberately
plans to evade or endure it; the occasional criminal thinks
little of the consequences of the act which is the expression
of his dominant idea; his crime is the " explosion " of an
instinct which reckons not with results. That the criminal
by passion or accident is not restrained by fear of punishment is evident from the very name of his group. He either
acts under the influence of passion which blinds him to
results or commits crime accidentally without knowledge of
wrong-doing. Probably the greatest value of punishment
is a sort of supplementary restraint to the moral sense in
those persons who would be criminals without it but with it
never are. We quote from Ferri a fitting summary of these
conclusions.

What we say is this. Punishment by itself, as a means of
repression, possesses a negative rather than a positive value;
not only because it has not the same influence on all anthropological types of criminals, but also because its use is rather
to preclude the serious mischief which would result from impunity than to convert, as some imagine it can, an anti-social
being into a social being. But impunity would lead to a
demoralization of the popular conscience in regard to crimes

[1] *Social Control,* p. 118.

and offences, to an increase of the profound lack of foresight in criminals, and to the removal of the impediment to fresh crimes during the term of incarceration.

That this purpose of restraint can be accomplished much more effectively and humanely by some other means than punishment will be demonstrated later.

The Interests of the Criminal. We are glad to have the assurance of an eminent writer that "the purely vindictive idea, though in Europe as in our own country still embodied in the law and tradition, is not as it once was the predominant feature in punishment; the idea of social protection dominates as it naturally must and leads to the segregation of the social offenders;" but we regret that so eminent a person added "it can as truly be said that reformation of prisoners is regarded as one of the ends through which every prison system must demonstrate its value and utility." [1] Conditions which warrant Mr. Barrows in making such a statement lead us to expect that, for many years to come, millions in state money and private funds will be expended in carrying on a well-nigh hopeless experiment which, if even moderately successful, must work untold injury upon subsequent generations. Science has shown and is showing more and more the narrowing field of reformation. In the introduction to his *Criminal Sociology,* Ferri writes:

No doubt the principle that punishment ought to have a reforming effect on the criminal survives as a redimentary tenet in nearly all the schools which concern themselves with crime. But this is only a secondary principle, and, as it were, the indirect object of punishment; and besides, the observations of anthropology, psychology and criminal statistics have finally disposed of it, having established the fact that, under any system

[1] S. J. Barrows, "European Prisons," *Charities,* Dec., '07.

of punishment, with the most severe or the most indulgent methods, there are always certain types of criminals, representing a large number of individuals, in regard to whom amendment is simply impossible, or very transitory, on account of their moral and organic degeneration. Nor must we forget that, since the natural roots of crime spring not only from the individual organism, but also in a large measure from the physical and social environment, correction of the individual is not sufficient to prevent relapse if we do not also, to the best of our ability, reform the social environment. The utility and duty of the reformation none the less survive, even for the positive school, whenever it is possible and for certain classes of criminals; but as a fundamental principle of a scientific theory, it has passed away.

Since we cannot hope to change materially the environment in response to the stimuli of which our criminal personality executes crime, our only hope lies in reforming the personality. The only way this can be done is by giving the criminal a new constitution, or, what is practically equal to it, to repair the one he has. We must despair of doing this except in special cases where natural defects causing criminality can be cured, or where the criminal is undoubtedly influenced by a particular environmental condition which can be changed or from which he can be permanently removed. We fear that such cases are rare and confined for the most part to the class of single offenders, to whom punishment is more often a bane than a blessing.

On the other hand, Dr. McKim writes: " Towards softening the flint-like obduracy of the moral imbecile all remedies remain unavailing. We may in some measure restrain but can never reform him. The general public has not yet grasped the truth now so well established that moral sense, like every other mental capacity, requires a fitting basis of brain structure, and that if this has never existed, or has

been destroyed by disease, a moral sense is impossible." [1]
Therefore the question resolves itself into a purely scientific one—medical science at that, or medico-legal at most.
The main interest of the criminal is that society protect
him from himself or from the reaction which would result
from his own activity. If for no other reason, he must be
restrained mercifully from expressing himself. Society
must do this, and do it humanely. The necessity is great
for the interests of society that it be moral in the treatment of its criminals. In order to be this, punishment must
be abandoned.

Since crime is the product of society existing in a given
environment, the criminal must be looked upon as the natural progeny of society under these conditions. In this
sense "society gets the criminality it deserves," *i. e.,* the
amount conditions call for.[2] Therefore criminals should
be treated as society now treats the dependent and defective,
in a manner consistent with our enlightened ideals of humanity and mercy. Society cannot afford to be vindictive
in its treatment of those poor unfortunates who are the
natural products of its own conditions.

So long have the accepted systems of criminal procedure
been based upon the idea of personal responsibility or freedom of the will that both structure and foundation must
ultimately perish together before methods in accord with
the findings of modern science can operate freely. Strange
as it may seem, the subject which was once declared to be
entirely within the province of philosophy can now be
treated without regard to the conclusions of the most profound philosophical discussions. The solution of the prob-

---

[1] *Op. cit.,* p. 21.

[2] Lacassagne, *Archives de l'anthropologie criminelle et des sciences
pénales.*

lem of moral responsibility is of no consequence to this work, hence it is not our intention to maintain either free will or determinism. To the social welfare, the question of freedom is not of the slightest consequence. If a man is free and deliberately wills to be unsocial, it is the right and the duty of society to protect itself against him; but that it should be cruel in so doing is neither a duty nor a right. Certainly nothing is gained by punishment. If the individual is restrained from crime by fear of punishment he is not free. Thus, incidentally, is seen the impossibility of proving freedom, and the unsatisfactory nature of a system based upon that doctrine. If a man is not free, if he is not at liberty to execute the power of choice or has no such power, then it is more than ever the duty of society to protect itself against him. If he is not free, punishment is not only futile but barbarous. Society thus puts itself in the absurd position of punishing a man for something he cannot help because he does not help it.

One thing has ever loomed dangerously in the way of absolute moral freedom as a criterion of guilt; that thing has been the ever-possible extenuating circumstance. An interesting chapter could be written upon the growth in numbers and importance of such circumstances. Insanity was once considered to be possession of the devil and because of this possession maniacs and imbeciles were punished and even put to death; but, with the conception of insanity as a malady—a disease—it passed to the opposite extreme and became one of the first and the most important conditions which rendered the subject irresponsible. To this have been added all forms of mental deficiency or alienation. Drunkenness has long been an extenuating circumstance in some quarters. In others it is considered a crime and punished with fine and imprisonment. Somnambulism and hypnotism are now presented as conditions wherein the subject has no control over his acts, and even the old standard, that ignorance of the law is no excuse, has been questioned with cause. The question of criminal intent early entered into the consideration. Responsibility was considered to be lessened when the crime was partly the result of accidental circumstances.

One of the early shocks which came to the system based upon the freedom of the will had its source in the development of statistical investigation. Discovery of the fact that a given population, subject to a not too great change of climatic conditions, in a given environment, would produce approximately the same amount of crime from year to year, led Quetelet to assert that " the budget of crime is an annual taxation paid with more precision than any other." With no unusual variations in temperature and harvests, even the number of certain kinds of crime such as murder and robbery could be calculated in advance with astonishing accuracy. The discoveries pointed significantly to the fact that crime was, in a large measure, the result of certain fixed conditions over which the individual had no control. Great progress in the perfection of statistical methods has established many facts beyond question. Suicides show a tendency to increase from January to June with the rise of temperature. The maximum figure for the year is reached in June when a decline sets in, reaching a minimum for the year in December.[1] Crimes against the person are more numerous in southern countries than crimes against property, while crimes against property exceed those against the person in northern latitudes. Crimes of violence and blood are more numerous in summer than in winter;[2] and crimes against property more numerous in winter than summer. In the light of these and numerous

---

[1] Mayo-Smith, *Statistics and Sociology.*   [2] *Ibid.*

similar statistical discoveries, together with the many striking results of experimental psychology, there is a growing
conviction on the part of scientific persons that man's
actions are determined, not by predestination of God but
by physical laws. " Before many years," says Dr. Giddings, " I believe we shall discover that at least 90 per cent
of human action is involuntary response to stimuli. Like
the summit of the ponderous iceberg, which only rears a
small portion of its bulk above the waves, the mind of man
seems to dominate and direct his activity; but in reality,
his conduct is the result of mighty forces little seen or
guessed at upon the surface." [1]

Science tells us that the natural state of matter is a state
of rest and that all motion is in response to force. This
force may be in the body moved or exterior to it. It may
move in response to expulsion or attraction. Where a body
is subjected to various forces its motion is a resultant of all
the forces and is different from what it would be if any
force were absent. The same holds true of human activity.
Man is at any moment the sum of all his previous experience, and his response to any stimulus is colored by that
experience. Thus the highly moral Christian gentleman
is not betrayed into rudeness by the grossest insult. We
might even go so far as to say that it would be impossible
for him to be rude. Long training, together with natural
tendencies, causes counter-stimuli to rise within him almost
simultaneously with the insult and determine his conduct.
The less-fortunately endowed and wholly uncultured individual swears volubly at a slight tread upon his toe. The
action of each is the natural reaction of personality in response to stimuli—his personality being the sum of his past
experience at the moment of action. Thus a person who

---

[1] *Unpublished lectures.*

has been reared with a profound belief in the sanctity of human life is restrained from becoming a murderer under any and all circumstances. Being what he is, murder to him is impossible. But another individual, reared in an atmosphere where revenge is a higher duty than obedience to the law, and having an inherent disposition to so regard it, kills his rival or a feud enemy as a natural expression of himself. He is no more free to choose any other course than is the keg of powder into which a live coal falls. Is the man, then, responsible? In the sense of being a free agent, perhaps not; but as the instrument which executes the deed, he is, most certainly. Responsibility, as Schopenhauer has long since said, supposes that an individual could have acted differently from the way he actually did act.[1] This is metaphysical responsibility. The only real responsibility is social responsibility. All men, whether free or not, no matter what their physical or mental condition, are responsible for their deeds to society. Society has a right to defend itself and preserve itself. Man is responsible because he lives in society, and only because of that social existence.[2] We are thus brought, as Hamon points out, to the acceptance of the old English legal maxim that everyone, whatever his state of consciousness, always acts at his own risk or peril. The insane and abnormal are, socially, necessarily responsible.[3]

Thus the question of moral freedom is not of the slightest interest. It is the result of response to stimuli which is of interest to society, not whether or not the individual could have responded differently from the way in which he did.

[1] A. Hamon, "La Résponsibilité" *Archives de l'anth. crim.*, quoted by Ellis.

[2] *Ibid.*   [3] *Ibid.*

CHAPTER V

Heredity and Environment

In the light of preceding conclusions our study of criminality is limited to the study of two fields. The first, and most important in the eyes of our criminal anthropologist friends, is the study of the criminal personality which responds to stimuli in a way intolerable to society. This involves us in an investigation of the complete history of the individual, including his inherited tastes and disposition, and the experiences he has encountered together with his bodily condition and, as far as possible, that of the ancestors from whom it was inherited. The second is the social and physical environment under which he has developed and in response to which he has acted in an anti-social manner. While the criminal is responsible to society for his acts, let not society forget that it is responsible for the criminal in a large measure and for many of the stimuli which have stimulated him to criminality. Thus heredity and environment divide between them the responsibility which was supposed to rest solely with the individual.

Heredity presents to us an individual, shaped and constituted in accordance with the immutable laws which dominate the realm of pre-natal life. By these same laws the nature of the response of the individual to environmental stimuli is also determined. Thus equipped he is turned over at birth to the mercies of the other great factor which will shape and complete his career. All the activities of his life are responses to its stimuli. By slow degrees the plastic thing which so recently yet so remotely began to exist is transformed by the pressure of its new dictator. It must be plastic or perish. As a result of this transformation the nature of its response is changed, but its essence is still the same. Its activity is still the expression of its self. Though modified, it is the same self as in the beginning.

An attempt to determine the relative amount of responsibility for crime which devolves upon each of these two factors would be fraught with innumerable difficulties and lead to no certain results. However, no one can read the works of the criminal anthropologists, or study criminals themselves, without acknowledging the tremendous importance of the part played by heredity. Its influence varies greatly in the classes of criminals. One could go almost as far as to assert that among the insane and born criminals it is entirely responsible for crime. We cannot conceive of any environment which would change their criminality. Of them Drähms writes:

The burden with which the congenital offender comes already laden, and from which he draws his inspirational forces, is purely congenital. It is the product of entailed inheritance from ancestral germ-plasms out of whose mysterious depths they are evolved, possessing all the potence that moulds the embryo into the image of the original, elaborating and imparting to it its very essence and individuality, even carrying in its current and inoculating that new life with the very germs of theft and murder already stirring in the blood of its progenitors ages back, and waiting but the call of opportunity to spring into sentient life in the scion, and expend itself at times in wanton joy at the incitation of the savage nature.

While the habitual and professional criminal cannot be said to be forced into crime by their natures, it is certain that they early discover that such a career is congenial to them and once they have tasted of its pleasures there is rarely ever any desire to live any other life. In the case of the occasional criminal heredity seems to play a small part because the amount of his crime is small, but in the very nature of the case it is almost entirely responsible for what there is. In the occasional criminal whose criminality is not so much of the " explosive " type, heredity plays a less important part. With him, as with the criminal by passion or accident, his hereditary tendency consists of the weakness of moral restraint together with a lack of comprehension of the consequences of his deed. In the latter group, practically the only hereditary factor consists of a lack of self-control, which, however, may be a powerful factor when a rigorous environment obtains.

As yet only crude efforts have been made to obtain the proportion of criminals in each class. If a large number of criminals could be successfully classified and the numbers in each class determined, a fair estimate could be given of the proportionate influence of heredity and environment. In all such considerations, as Dr. McKim says, it must be clearly understood that crime cannot be hereditary but merely the tendency to crime. The same might be said of disease, between which and heredity the relation is very close. Defective conduct, he continues, " has its root in defective brain action, which is dependent upon defective brain structure, and this may be congenital or acquired—usually through morbid tendencies transmitted by inheritance. Upon heredity, disease and degeneracy are in a great degree dependent; these are the roots from which spring abnormal tendencies and deficient self-restraint. Criminality, then, the noxious flower of this twofold growth, is essentially a manifestation of heredity."

Statistics are not wanting to show the high proportion of disease, insanity and alcoholism in parents of criminals.

Numerous efforts have been made to account for crime as the direct result of alcoholism, of which, probably the most reasonable and thoroughgoing is an article by Dr. Henry Smith Williams in the December (1908) number of *McClure's Magazine*. Dr. Williams' array of authorities includes for this country, the latest annual report of the New York State Commission in Lunacy, and the reports of alcoholic experiments upon the tissues of the brain and nervous system of animals by Dr. Berkly and Dr. Friedenwald of Johns Hopkins; for England and Wales, Dr. Robert Jones and Dr. Theodore B. Hyslop, Physician and Superintendent to the Royal Hospitals of the Bridewell and " Bedlam "; for Scotland, Dr. Clouston, Superintendent of the Royal Edinburg Asylum, and Dr. Tuke of the Royal Dundee Asylum. He gives official figures prepared by Dr. Legrain of the Asylum of St. Anne in Paris, by Dr. Tilkowsky for the asylums in Vienna, and Drs. Baer, Laquer, Nasse, Jung, Pelham, and Stark for different cities of the German Empire. These investigators, gathering their facts from reluctant friends and relatives of insane patients, testify that alcohol is everywhere the prime causative factor in from 25 per cent to 50 per cent of all cases of insanity.

Dr. Williams quotes the Lord Chief Justice of England as saying that, if sifted, nine-tenths of the crime of England and Wales could be traced to drink. The condition which induced the crime was ascribed to alcohol in 84 per cent of all criminals investigated by the Massachusetts Bureau of Labor Statistics. In seventeen prisons and reformatories of twelve states the Committee of Fifty found that half the graver crimes were committed by persons under the influence of intoxicants. Mr. Dugdale found over 40 per cent of the first-term men in Sing Sing and Auburn Prisons to be habitual drunkards. Statistics of like import are produced for Great Britain and Continental Europe—including, especially, the nations which consume light wines and beers. The reports of charitable institutions estimate that two-fifths of the pauper and one-half of the dependent children in this country and abroad owe their condition to the demoralizing influence of drink.

At the close of a review of Mr. Williams' article in the *New York Times* of November 27, 1908, we find the following comment: "Dr. Williams' citations serve to heighten the popular impression that alcohol is directly responsible for much poverty, insanity, and crime. A study of the reasons why alcoholic beverages are indulged in, even moderately, might show that the indulgence *is a symptom as well as a cause* of evil and lies outside the pale of prohibitive legislation." [1] No amount of authoritative statements could prove the assertion that alcoholism is the direct cause of crime. The most significant fact suggested by these writers is that hinted at in the above editorial. While the incident of drunkenness or the effect of constant indulgence may aid materially in the commission of crime, dipsomania and criminality are equally significant effects and evidence of the real state of affairs—a hereditary taint in the individual. Mr. Dugdale, quoted above, says that such investigations tend to show that certain diseases and mental disorders precede the appetite for stimulants, and that the true cause of their use is the antecedent hereditary or induced physical exhaustion.

When insanity and alcoholism are combined in the parents a rich and awful legacy of degeneration is left to the offspring. Thus, one among many instances, Morel quotes a case in which the father was alcoholic, the mother insane, and of the five children one committed suicide, two became convicts, one daughter was mad and another an imbecile. Carefully-drawn statistics of the 4000 criminals who have

[1] *Italics mine.*

passed through Elmira, New York, show drunkenness clearly existing in the parents of about 30 per cent and probably very many more.[1]

The influence of heredity cannot always be said to be a passing-on of developed conditions which express themselves in crime. Sometimes, says Ellis, a generation is merely one stage in the progressive degeneration of a family. Sometimes crime seems to be the method by which the degenerating organism seeks to escape from an insane taint in the parents. Of the inmates in the Elmira Reformatory nearly twelve per cent have been of insane or epileptic heredity. Of 233 prisoners at Auburn, N. Y., 23.03 per cent were clearly of neurotic origin. Marro, who has examined the matter very carefully, found the proportion affected by supposedly hereditary diseases to be 77 per cent, and by taking into consideration a large range of abnormal characters in the parents, the proportion of criminals with bad heredity rose to 90 per cent. Tarde asserts that 46 per cent of delinquents have had alcoholic parents, and adding those who have had epileptic and hysterical parents and those whose parents were themselves criminals, he raises the proportion of criminals with bad heredity to 90 per cent, corroborating Marro's figures quoted above.[2] Dugdale noted that out of 233 criminals in Elmira, 49 were clearly neurotic, 95 were orphans, 40 came from criminal families, 52 from pauper stock, 99 from itinerant families, and 91 were dipsomaniacs. It is interesting to notice that of the 42 criminals who committed crimes against the person 17, over two-fifths, were neurotic, and that of the 15 convicted of rape or attempt to rape over one-half were neurotic, one-third were orphans, two-fifths drunkards.[3]

[1] Ellis, *op. cit.*, p. 110.   [2] *La philosophie pénale*, p. 177.
[3] *The Jukes*, chart.

Sometimes the criminal tradition is carried on through many generations and with great skill, a kind of professional cast being formed. Ellis cites the Johnston family of counterfeiters as an example of this. The grandfather was a counterfeiter in his day and the next generation was well known to the police; in the third generation criminal audacity and skill appear to have reached a very high degree in seven brothers and sisters, one of them, especially, being considered one of the most expert counterfeiters of the day. He spent a large part of his life in various prisons.

In addition to numerous instances of such criminal families mentioned in current works on crime, we have several interesting works devoted entirely to the study of individual families. McCulloch has given us a graphic description of two such families which we wish to reproduce in part.[1]

Ben Ishmael had eight children—five sons and three daughters. Some of the descendants are now living in Kentucky, and are prosperous, well-regarded citizens. One son, named John, married a half-breed woman and moved to Marion County, Indiana, about 1840. He was diseased and could go no further. He had seven children, of whom two were left in Kentucky, one was lost sight of, and one remained unmarried. The remaining three sons married three sisters *from a pauper family* named Smith.[2] These had children of whom thirty are now living in the fifth generation. Since 1840 this family has had a pauper record. They have been in the almshouse, the house of refuge, the woman's reformatory, the penitentiaries, and have received continuous aid from the township. They are intermarried with other members of this group and with over 200 other families. In this family history are murders, a large number of illegitimates and prostitutes. They

---

[1] *The Tribe of Ishmael.*   *Italics mine.*

are generally diseased. The children die young. They live by petty stealing, begging and ash-gathering. In summer they " gipsy " or travel in wagons east and west. In the fall they return. They have been known to live in hollow trees on river bottoms or in empty houses.

In the Owen family of Kentucky there were originally four children of whom two have been traced, William and Brook. William had three children who raised pauper families. One son of the third generation died in the penitentiary; a daughter in the fourth generation was a prostitute with two illegitimate children. Another son in the third generation had a penitentiary record and died of delirium tremens. There have been several murders, and a continuous pauper and criminal record. An illegitimate half-breed Canadian woman enters this family. There is much prostitution but little intemperance.

Brook had a son John who was a Presbyterian minister He raised a family of fourteen illegitimate children. Ten of these moved to Indiana and three of them raised illegitimate families in the fourth generation; and of these two daughters and a son have illegitimate children in the fifth generation.

Probably the most interesting work of this nature is that of Dugdale, *The Jukes*. This is a study of a remarkable family which originated, as far as is known, about the middle of the eighteenth century in a wild and almost inaccessible rocky region in the State of New York. The earliest direct ancestor studied was born of early Dutch settlers about 1720-1740. He lived the life of a back-woodsman, was a hard drinker and averse to steady labor. He lived to an extreme old age and became blind, leaving at his death a numerous progeny more or less illegitimate. Two of his sons married two out of a more or less illegitimate family of five sisters. These sisters are the Jukes. The name is a fictitious one given them by the author. Their descendants constitute the largest criminal family known to history. Mr. Dugdale traced the descendants of these sisters through five generations. The number thus traced reached 709. The real aggregate at the time of the investigation (1877) was probably 1200 and no doubt now exceeds twice that number. Following is a description of their manner of living in Mr. Dugdale's own words:

Most of the ancestors were squatters on the soil, and in some instances have become owners by tax-title or by occupancy. They lived in log or stone houses similar to slave hovels, all ages, sexes, relations, and strangers "bunking" indiscriminately. One form of this bunking has been described to me. During the winter the inmates lie on the floor strewn with straw or rushes like so many radii to the hearth, the embers of the fire forming a center toward which their feet focus for warmth. This proximity, where not producing illicit relations, must often have involved an atmosphere of suggestiveness fatal to habits of chastity.

Of the 162 women of this stock, 84 were harlots, or 52.4 per cent. Of the 64 women who were of mixed blood, 28 were harlots, over 41.76 per cent. Out of 475 children, 82 were illegitimate, or 23.5 per cent. Out of 45 inebriates only three were healthy, ten were diseased, and twenty-nine were licentious. At the close of the study Mr. Dugdale gives an interesting estimate of the fearful cost of this family to society in time, money, and human lives. "Over a million and a quarter dollars loss in seventy-five years caused by a single family 1200 strong, without reckoning the price paid for whiskey, or taking into account the entailment of pauperism and crime of the survivors in succeeding generations, and the incurable disease, idiocy and insanity growing out of this debauchery, and reaching further than we can calculate."

From the study of such records one derives an ever-increasing appreciation of the importance of the inherited organism. The immensity of this importance is not yet appreciated. Even in the last group of our classification, where heredity plays the smallest part of any of the groups, we are persuaded that we have not, as yet, the faintest conception of the immense part played by inherited disposition (which is determined by inherited organism) in determining the nature of response to stimuli.

Even popularly speaking it is generally conceded that we inherit tastes, habits, diseases, or tendency to diseases, physical characteristics, *etc.;* why not criminal tendencies as well? After arriving at practically these conclusions Mr. Maudsley writes: " If the secrets of their natures were laid open, how many perverse and wrong-headed persons, whose lives have been a calamity to themselves and others, how many of the depraved characters in history, whose careers have been a cruel chastisement to mankind, would be found to have owed their fates to some morbid predisposition!" [1]

While heredity plays an enormous part in all the groups of our classification, there is a growing conviction that environment plays an important part in but three of them. One cannot doubt the importance of environment in special cases. No doubt a large majority of single offenders are so because of environmental conditions.

To the insane or born criminal, environment affords merely an opportunity for him to express himself. He would find this in any environment. In a large majority of cases where environment plays an important rôle its work is done at an early age after which it becomes merely opportunity or occasion as in the case of the insane and born criminal. Its most dominant effects are those made

[1] *Op. cit.*, p. 59.

upon the physical or mental constitution of the individual. Such effects upon grown people are very slight. The effects of temporary association upon adults are merely incidental: the permanent associations are largely the result of the individual's disposition. As a result of this, environment is of practically no importance to professional or habitual criminals after a certain age. It played its greatest rôle in their production. In our sixth group, that of criminals by passion or accident, environment has little or no part in the very nature of the case. The accidental circumstances which make the one a criminal, the incidental causes of uncontrollable passion in the other can occur with equal frequency and facility in any environment, either good or bad. A practically unanswerable question is put to those who attribute crime to the influence of social environment by Ferri in the following terms:

In fact, if crime were the exclusive product of the social environment, how could one explain the familiar fact that in the same social environment, and in identical circumstances of poverty, abandonment, lack of education, sixty per cent do not commit crimes, and of the forty, five prefer suicide, five go mad, five simply become beggars or tramps not dangerous to society, whilst the remaining twenty-five actually commit crimes? And amongst the latter, while some go no further than theft without violence, why do others commit theft with violence, and even kill their victim outright, before he offers resistance, or threatens them, or calls for help, and this with no other object than gain?[1]

Notwithstanding the wide experience of social workers, we cannot accept their well-nigh unanimous conclusions that amelioration of social conditions is possible to a sufficient extent to materially lessen the amount of crime. Even if it were possible by one stroke to exterminate the slums,

[1] *Op. cit.*, p. 56.

it would be found useless to hope for continued beneficent results. If it were possible to readjust society so that each individual were given an equally favorable social environment with every other individual the capable and strong would rise above, the incapable and weak would sink below, the artificial level thus established. The particularly weak and deficient would sink to the extreme depths. The dregs of humanity would create new slums. True to the continuous effort of the race to improve itself, numerous superior individuals would appear among these as they do now, and philanthropists would make numerous and mostly unscientific efforts, as they do now, to save them, even at the expense of perpetuating numerous unfit brothers and sisters. The dregs cannot be kept from going to the bottom except by continual stirring, a process both expensive and disastrous.

The real function of environment is to give heredity full sway. All efforts to interfere with conditions which are the result of fundamental laws without a thorough understanding of those laws and scientific provision to evade the consequences of them must not end in failure only but disaster as well. Therefore an effort to remedy environmental conditions for individuals whose heredity has determined their fate is not an ignorant waste only, but courts calamity if not tragedy. The conviction that what is good for a majority of a group is not necessarily good for all the individuals in that group is growing firmer daily. Thirty years ago Maudsley wrote:

There are in reality many persons who, without being actually imbecile or insane, are of lower moral responsibility than the average of mankind; they have been taught the same lessons as the rest of mankind, and have a full theoretical knowledge of them, but they have not really assimilated them; the principles inculcated never gained that hold of their minds which they gain in a sound and well-constituted nature. After all that can be said, an individual's nature will only assimilate, that is, will only make of the same kind with itself, what is fitted to further its special development, and this it will by a natural affinity, find in the conditions of its life. To the end of the chapter of life the man will feel, think, and act according to his kind. The wicked are not wicked by the deliberate choice of the advantages of wickedness, which are a delusion, or the pleasures of wickedness, which are a snare, but by an inclination of their natures which makes the evil good to them and the good evil.

As Maudsley led the opinion of his time, Tarde now ventures ahead of present-day scientific tendencies. He thinks that if one examined hundreds of thousands of judges, lawyers, laborers, musicians, taken at random and in various countries, noting their different characters, craniometric, algometric, sphygmographic, graphologic, photographic, and so on, as Lombroso has examined hundreds and thousands of criminals, it is extremely probable that we should find facts no less surprising.[1]

We have to get away from the idea that a little readjustment of conditions would solve our social problems. Things are what they are as a natural result of abiding causes. The criminal is no more unnatural than the honest man. He seems a monster to us because of his rarity and the importance of his activity. As it is natural, says Drähms, for a normally-constituted and well-balanced youth, springing from a sound stock with an unbiased heredity and nourished by a favorable environment, to develop naturally into right doing, and to grow up under favorable surroundings into a healthy, law-abiding manhood; so it is equally in accordance with the irrevocable logic of things that the ill-equipped and abnormally-engendered youth, re-enforced by

[1] *La Criminalitie comparée*, p. 51.

vicious environment, should result in a distinctive moral anomaly and physical degenerate.

As long as degeneration, from whatever cause, continues, depraved heredity will present us with criminals. As long as criminals exist environment must play its active and important part in the drama of crime. Conditions which rob environment of its power to figure in crime are as remote as they are utopian. Much is hoped for through education, but where the conditions are the worst the detrimental features of our school system are the most disastrous. Admitting all the possibilities of changed social conditions and modified educational methods, we must not forget, that, to a great extent, the individual life is determined before social environment can have much influence. We are daily confronted with the unhappy spectacle of persons endowed by their ancestors with physical or mental qualities which will remain forever a hopeless handicap upon their prospects in life. Evidence is not wanting to show the tremendous importance of the conditions governing prenatal life. If the truth were known, no doubt many a man would rightly ascribe the wreck of his existence to the fact that his advent into the world was an undesired event.

As long as the struggle for existence continues, heredity, ably seconded by environment, will continue to produce the criminal. But the proportion of criminals that are produced by the struggle alone is small if we subtract from the total all descendants of criminal, alien, and pauper stocks. Such a remedy is possible, and, we believe, the time is not far remote when criminality may be reduced to the amount of crime committed by the residue which settles to the bottom of each succeeding generation. While the methods of hastening that time which are suggested in the remaining chapters of this work may not be utilized directly, we hope that they will suggest others which will accomplish the much-desired result.

CHAPTER VI

The Death Penalty

WHAT is commonly termed the "death penalty" and "capital punishment" has its germs far back of the time when the ideas embodied in "penalty" and "punishment" had their birth. Its original expression was extermination. Among animals, killing of members of their own kind seldom occurs except among males. The stranger, as among savages, is an enemy and he is destroyed or cowed by the ruler of the group who by his strength has constituted himself lord over it. This is not punishment nor the infliction of a penalty, yet unquestionably both of these ideas arise from this. Probably the earliest form of either of these appears in one of three forms. Occasionally an effort is made by some cowed male who has been permitted to remain in the group, to obtain the mastery over his hated oppressor. If he is unsuccessful his extermination is altogether likely. Again, some act on the part of one of his subjects arouses the ruler to a fatal passion or a quarrel among members of the group over food, or young, or even over a particular resting place may result in death of one of them. Another instance, and probably the most definite one, frequently occurs when, the whole group being threatened from without, some member whose indiscreet action imperils the whole is visited with swift death by his own kindred. In all such instances the destroyed individual is looked upon for the time being as an enemy. The only object is extermination in response to the instinct of

self-preservation. Among animals this is exceeded in rare
cases only. Bees punish non-workers with death in time
of famine, and some such conduct is observed among ants.
Storks have been said to punish adulterous members of their
groups with death, but there is very little corroboration of
such statements. We must come far over into the life of
man before we find death inflicted as a punishment or penalty for certain acts or omissions to act.

The idea of retribution probably grew out of religion.
It was long a powerful weapon in the hands of priests for
demanding respect and obedience to mandates of their various gods. From such cults, which long antedated civil
society, it was brought over into the earliest codes but does
not lose its religious nature till ages after. In many places
where it is still practiced it is looked upon as the judgment
of Almighty God.

Capital punishment, as such, presents the absurd paradox
of a punishment raised to its severest terms, where it ceases
to punish. Therefore the death penalty is a better word.
No doubt the deterrent idea became attached to this penalty early in the history of the human race, coming, parallel
with the idea of punishment, from the priesthood. In order
to frighten men into obedience to the deities they served
they threatened them with the direst calamity known to them
—death. Because of the well-nigh universal ideas of more
or less terrible fates awaiting individuals after death, especially individuals who were in disfavor with the gods, such
threats were powerful deterrents, and the ceremony of execution was made as pompous and imposing as possible to
add to its deterrent power. Thus we have coming down
to us side by side the idea of a death penalty as a protection
to society against the immediate offender by his extermination and the idea of the utility of the dread penalty as a

means of deterring prospective offenders. Late in the development of the race the deterrent idea passes over into an idea of social protection. In all probability, it will soon be, if it is not at present, the dominant idea in capital punishment. Du Cane cites an instance of a Heath judge who said to a horsethief he had just condemned to the gallows: " You are sentenced to be hanged, not because you stole the horse, but in order to prevent others from stealing horses." [1]

Desperate efforts to make the death penalty a deterrent were responsible for some of the blackest pages in the history of the English people. With this end in view all sorts of gruesome methods of execution were resorted to. Blackstone tells us that " among the variety of actions which men are daily liable to commit, no less than one hundred and sixty have been (1769) declared by act of Parliament to be felonies without benefit of clergy " (punishable by death).[2] The death penalty was carried out by hanging, burning or the axe and, during a few years of Henry VIII's reign, boiling to death was made lawful for poisoning Burning was the punishment for heresy and for petty treason. A woman was burned for counterfeiting in 1788. Hanging was substituted for burning in 1790. Some time prior to this burning was mercifully preceded by hanging.

Sir S. Romilly tried from 1810 to 1818 to have pocket-picking over one shilling and stealing taken out of capital offenses. He was at last successful. In 1833 a child of nine years was sentenced to be hanged for breaking in a patched window with a stick and stealing two pence worth of paint, but the sentence was not executed. From 1832 to 1844 no one was hanged for any other crime than murder.

[1] " *Punishment and Prevention of Crime,*" p. 2.
[2] *Commentaries,* 2nd ed.

Gradually the fact was being forced upon the minds of the authorities that capital punishment was not reducing crime. The desperate efforts of the past one hundred years had been the result of ignorant fears that the foundations of society would be overthrown. The ever-increasing futility of more and more violent repressive measures roused the country to a frenzy which deluged the land with blood. Gradually the reaction came, and has continued to this day.

This change in the attitude of criminal justice toward the death penalty has without doubt been due to the growing conviction that it does not deter, together with the development of the humane instinct in those who have made and enforced the laws dealing with crime. The deterrent value of the death penalty certainly is not its great value McDonald tells us that of one hundred and seventy-seven persons condemned to death who had been studied, only three had not been present at other executions. The only value, then, which attaches to the death penalty is the extermination of a person who is a continuous menace to society both in his activity and his power to reproduce his kind. Let us study these phases separately. The latter one will be considered in the chapter on Propagation.

What are the advantages of the death penalty? Two at least are apparent and go far to keep up a practice which has long bade fair to disappear. When practiced in a humane manner it is without doubt the most merciful to the prisoner. The long waiting of the life prisoner, first cheered by hoping against hope, transforms hope into despair, the man into the brute, and, when once this is done, we have before us the most horrible spectacle imaginable— a living death. On the other hand, under the present penal system the death penalty affords the cheapest and safest method of protecting society. Under our present system, in which imprisonment for a term of years is the penalty for certain forms of murder, great numbers of men are liberated from our penitentiaries annually who are as much murderers at their liberation as at their condemnation. Even when the sentence is for life, the susceptibility of governors to influence by popular petitions constantly threatens the community with the release of the most villainous of convicts, especially when they have served a long sentence and the humane instincts of the pardoner persuade him that the man has been punished enough. Added to this is the constant danger of escape, which often happens, even with our highly-developed system of detention. Those who escape are almost invariably the most hardened and desperate criminals who too often, even though recaptured, leave a trail of blood and violence to mark the scene of their freedom. Such occurrences lead some to say, with a German contemporary, that the death penalty is the only form of punishment for cold-blooded and premeditated murder.[1] Such offenders are almost invariably born criminals. Concerning these, Ferri says:

For born criminals, since, as Dr. Maudsley says, we are face to face, if not exactly with a degenerate species, at least with a degenerate variety of the human species, and the problem is to diminish their number as much as possible, a preliminary question at once arises, namely, whether the penalty of death is not the most suitable and efficacious form of social defence against the anti-social class, when they commit crimes of great gravity.[2]

Such considerations, however, lead to the question, Are there not other individuals who are as much a menace to the community as the cold-blooded murderer? Are we not somewhat influenced in his case by the spirit of retaliation? Is not, for instance, the sexual pervert, or the perpetrator

[1] Krauss, *Die Psychologie des Verbrechens.*   [2] *Op. cit.*, p. 238.

of arson liable to bring disaster upon an individual or a
community far more grievous than the sudden death of a
single victim? Is not the father of criminals, who is such
by reason of degeneration or debauch, as much a menace to
society by reason of his potential criminality as any one of
his depraved progeny? Such being the case, are we not
inconsistent when we support and pamper the one in an
institution of mercy and hang the other whose life our misguided sympathy has made possible? If the death penalty
is practiced at all, should it not be carried out logically for
the extermination of all criminals who are proved to be a
continual menace, and not merely for a few special cases?
In answer to such questions as these, Dr. McKim has
worked out one of the clearest and most consistent pleas
for the improvement of the race that has ever been produced. After a careful investigation of the hereditary
nature of delinquents and defectives, if not of dependents,
he boldly asserts that in order to save the race from degeneration we must resort to an artificial selective process. He
writes: " in the case of idiots and of many imbeciles, epileptics, and habitual drunkards and criminals, we can pre-
dict so surely a life of wretchedness for the individual and
of injury to the public weal that, authority being granted, we
might at once with a clear conscience decree their extinction." [1] Carrying out the idea of social protection, he
would thus exterminate the following groups: 1, all idiots;
2, the greater number of imbeciles—certainly moral imbeciles; 3, the majority of epileptics; 4, drunkards who have
become a menace to posterity; 5, dangerous criminals, including all the insane, born, habitual and professional criminals; 6, grossly defective dependents. Nor can we accuse
him of harshness or cruelty. Throughout his work he

[1] *Op. cit.*, p. 249.

maintains an attitude of pity for the persons he condemns, but feels forced to advocate his remedy in the name of generations yet unborn. Startling as Dr. McKim's conclusions are, we feel compelled, after an investigation of the subject, to accept them, but we cannot accept his remedy. He is quite correct that it is nature's way of keeping a stock healthy and robust, but to return to it now by violence would be a disaster to the race far more serious than its prospective degeneration. The shock to the moral sense of society as a whole would be a misfortune far outweighing the advantages of elimination. It is true that we have a large group of entirely humane scholars who would survive the shock and persist in their humanity, but the day of Dr. McKim's " enlightened pity " is so far remote that the prospect of its arriving in time to save us from degeneration on account of the objects of that pity are not great. To the great mass of people who are humane enough to respond to the general demand for sympathy and brotherly kindness, such a procedure would be a shock from which they would not recover for ages to come.

Society is better for objects of altruism. They have played an important part in the development of the humane instinct. The value of the ideal of Jesus to the race has been and will always continue to be its finding of self in the consideration of the welfare of others. But even philanthropy becomes scientific. The same code which commended the good Samaritan two thousand years ago, to-day cleans up the road to Jericho and, by eliminating the robbers and making their return impossible, leaves the good Samaritan free to use his talents in some other occupation. He now occupies an important seat on the committee of public safety.[1] But the unfortunate man who " went down to Jeri-

[1] Patten, *The New Basis of Civilization.*

cho " has served his purpose. In ministering to the individual, humanity has learned how to minister to the race. The religion of the future will be one in which the love for one's brother has been merged into the love for humanity. The three years of Jesus' ministry might be used as a type of the progress of the ideal he lived for. Starting his ministry by helping individuals and teaching a few, he gradually realized that his field was broader and in order to be true to his larger vision he stopped not at the cross lest he be untrue to his ideal.

But the work of humanizing the race began ages before when the wandering horde stopped in its travels to heed the cry of the helpless.[1] Society always protected the young. Where this was not done society was not possible on any considerable scale. In this lay the possibilities of all future development. The wandering band of animals protected its young because of inherent instincts which made them social, but the weaklings and the aged, the infirm and crippled were left on the trail to die of starvation or perish at the hands of their natural enemies. Even savages practice the killing or deserting of their aged and infirm and the destruction of unpromising young. But while the stock was improved in this manner it was at the expense of the possibility of the nobler sentiments which characterize humanity. For long ages the old and infirm fell out of the ranks and perished in silence; but as the organic sympathy which bound them together became more and more a consciousness of kind the struggle on the part of the weaklings to keep in the ranks became more and more desperate and it was not given over without an anguished cry for assistance. For still longer ages the cry was unheeded. but through all this time the instinctive affection for the

[1] F. H. Giddings, *Unpublished Lectures.*

young strengthened and expanded until it included with its direct object the older members of the immediate group. Here are the rudiments of love and here the moral sentiments are born.[1] When this family affection is sufficiently developed in the group to make it conscious of the cry of the helpless we might say that humanity is conceived. When it is sufficiently developed to stay the progress of the group in order to lend a helping hand to the one who would have perished without it, humanity is born.[2] The passage from savagery to philanthropy begins when the group begins to care for its weaklings instead of deserting or destroying them.

This new thing born into the world has had a checkered history. In spite of countless checks and reverses it has so sufficiently developed in our time to declare that " every society upon arriving at a certain stage of civilization finds that it is positively necessary for its own sake, that is to say, for the satisfaction of its own humanity, and for the due performance of the purpose for which society exists, to provide that no person, no matter what has been his life, or what may be the consequences, shall perish for want of bare necessities of existence." [3] But, as in the animal kingdom, no creature is born without imperiling the life of its parent, so in this unnamed realm, this birth was fraught with many perils. When the group stopped to aid the helpless member, the wise law, which nature had provided for the purpose of developing a perfect stock, was violated. Those inferior and deformed individuals who were marked for extermination were nourished and supported and thus permitted to perpetuate an inferior stock with infinite multi-

---

[1] Sutherland, *op. cit.*

[2] F. H. Giddings, *Unpublished Lectures.*

[3] Fowle,*The Poor Law,* p. 10.

plications and ramifications in succeeding generations. In an effort to be kind to a few individuals in their own generation they provided untold misery for their posterity. Being a progeny of instinct this trait has seldom appealed to reason and has expressed itself in all sorts of disastrous ways. At present we see it making frantic and expensive effort to patch up the wrecks of humanity that they may propagate a few more wrecks for the next generation of enthusiasts to expend their overflowing sympathies upon. Foundling babies, who by the very nature of their cases are the offspring of degenerate or criminal parents, are saved alive and guaranteed a future while thousands of well-bred and perfectly-formed children waste away and die because of malnutrition on the part of their mothers or because of conditions forced upon them by an undiscriminating educational system. Elaborate pains are taken to force upon truants and juvenile delinquents technical education while the children of good parents have to forge out their careers by main strength and awkwardness. Misguided sentimentalists waste their substance in bestowing gifts of food and clothing upon the first persons encountered, thus encouraging pauperism and offering a reward for shiftlessness. Bejeweled donors crush street gamins under their motor wheels while hurrying to a meeting of the society for the prevention of cruelty to animals and dying leave fortunes for the perpetuation of institutions for the care of homeless cats.

From the degenerate masses of humanity perpetuated and multiplied by misguided sympathy of a similar sort come our criminals. We tried at one time to exterminate them by the death penalty. Time has shown that this is not the remedy to take the place of the natural process our humane instincts have made void. As Dr. Allison says, if capital punishment fails to protect society, if, as maintained by many experts, it increases criminality, then those states that practice capital punishment are committing a murderous blunder. The ends of society can be conserved by a less strenuous means than extermination and at the same time objects of scientific philanthropy be spared sufficient to guarantee the continued development of the humane instinct without the present menace to the race.

CHAPTER VII

THE PRISON SYSTEM

NEXT to the word death, the word prison has, perhaps, the most terrible significance for all people who have knowledge of the idea expressed by it. Personal liberty, by those people who have possessed the merest shreds of it under tyrannical governments, as well as by the citizens of the most utopian republics, has been looked upon as a divine right, a God-given heritage, to be deprived of which was the direst calamity short of death. For this reason, and on account of a mass of popular ideas that have grown up, probably not without cause, about the prison, the idea of it is associated with the few other great and awful calamities which hover threateningly near the borders of human experience. Children are frightened by it, women shrink from the thought of it, and strong men blanch at the possibility and faint at the certainty of it for them. Thus among oppressed peoples the prison becomes the most hated of institutions, and the first act of the Paris mob upon finding itself free from the tyrant was to destroy the Bastile.

Short-sighted as the masses have ever been, they conceive of an ideal land where prisons do not exist, unless for their enemies, not discerning that prisons are a result of a fundamental condition of society. True there was a time when there were no prisons, but that time was not the blissful state conceived of by utopian dreamers. There was no prison for our remote ancestors, but it was not because there was no crime; swift death quickly and con-

veniently prevented the necessity for such an institution
At less remote periods culprits were flogged, tortured, be-
reft of property or outlawed when not executed; but retention " in durance vile " was not yet conceived of.

There is no doubt that many readers will be surprised to
learn that the prison was in use long before it had any association with crime. Not until comparatively recent times
were social offenders incarcerated. The first occupant of the
prison was the captive taken from another tribe, or a prisoner of war; and dark and forbidding as the history of
the prison has been, it has not yet successfully vied with
the institutions which brought it forth. It is the hybrid
progeny of the unholy alliance of religion and cannibalism.

In primitive warfare, men fought to the death, neither
asking nor showing mercy. The struggle for existence was
without any actuating motive other than self or social defense. All strangers were enemies to be destroyed; and
so strong was this instinct of self-protection grounded
in the race that it survives to-day in the most highly civilized nations in the form of antipathy for foreigners, especially members of another race. Captives are not taken in
war without a motive, and this was lacking in primitive
warfare. The possibility that vanquished enemies were
saved alive as trophies of prowess or bravery has been suggested; but a part of the slain enemy long answered this
purpose. When life was so precarious and food scarce, a
living victim was too cumbersome and expensive to keep:
necklaces or bracelets of teeth, skulls mounted on poles, as
in the case of certain African tribes, and locks of hair, cut
scalp and all from the bleeding victim, a well-known custom of the American Indians, served the purpose much
more conveniently and just as effectually. Captives were
not taken alive from the field of battle until a use for them

arose. Such a use, in due time, appears from a surprising source.

Early in the history of man, sometime in the far-distant dawn of human existence, probably under circumstances of direst want, it was discovered that human flesh was not only a food but a delicacy. The remoteness of this discovery is incalculable; but cannibalism is hinted at in almost all our earliest traditions, a fact which testifies to a custom once generally in practice, and which has survived in historic times in many savage tribes, in some instances down to our own time.[1] Wherever the discovery led to the general practice of eating human flesh, a feast followed a battle, the victors gorging themselves upon the slain. It is improbable, however, that this led to the taking of captives until another custom arose, growing out of cannibalism, namely, the offering of human sacrifice to the gods.

It is probable that several theorists are correct about the origin, or the origins, of religion. It probably arose from several sources on account of a sort of religious instinct, or an inherent feeling of awe and reverence in the presence of the terrible, the sublime, or the unknown and unknowable. Mr. Spencer finds a possible cause for it in the origin of the conception of a dual self, growing out of the appearance of reflections in clear water and smooth surfaces, the echo, dreams, and the return of consciousness after coma from blows or sickness. From the observance of such things as these man arrived at a conception of another world in which his other self lives on after death.[2]

Whether this is a true explanation of the origin of religion or not, it is, at least, an explanation of the origin of a certain form of religion, namely, ancestor worship, the phase of religion with which we come in contact at this point in our explanation of the probable origin of the prison.

[1] Darling, *Anthropophagy*.   [2] *Principles of Sociology*, vol. ii, pt. i.

Since a great chieftain was supposed to live on and rule after his death, his survivors sought to appease his anger or obtain his favor by offering in sacrifice to his spirit those things which they knew were especially acceptable to him during his corporeal existence. If he had been a great cannibal during his life, human flesh was sacrificed to him after his death. Long after, when remoteness and the continual augmentation of his prowess and virtues in traditional lore had raised him to the dignity of the one great ancestor of the people and the greatest of their ancestral gods, he was supposed to feed upon the souls of the sacrificed while the priests feasted upon the bodies.

Thus arose a motive for taking captives in war, and men conquered in battle were spared alive for this gruesome purpose. Bound and carried, or tied to their captors and led, they were taken to the villages of the victors and sacrificed to the ancestral spirits; and, after the system of worship was sufficiently developed to require worship or sacrifice on stated occasions, victims were kept from time of capture until the next day of sacrifice in rude stockades or rocky caverns—the first prisons. It has been suggested that the usefulness of the captives as servants was discovered during this period of detention and that slavery originated thus. Certain it is that when war did not offer victims for sacrifice, slaves were substituted, and in some instances, wives of the dead chief, if his death were recent.

When once the stockade and rocky cavern, and their successor, the dungeon, were established, the prison, in some form or other, never disappeared from the history of the human race. When peace with external enemies began to take the place of warfare, and the survivor of cannibalism, human sacrifice, gave place to slain beasts or a more spiritual form of worship, the prison did not fall into decay for want of occupants. In the place of its vanquished savage, fattening for sacrifice, are fettered hosts of dethroned monarchs, frustrated usurpers and traitors, dangerous subjects and rival aspirants for power. Meanwhile the established religion fills its section to overflowing with heretics and dissenters, and vile infidels, cursed of God. So firmly is the prison ingrafted into the social system that it still flourishes in our most enlightened civilizations, though the awakened human conscience is becoming restive under its galling weight. Small wonder that but a few courageous spirits have dared to cry out or take up pen to urge its extermination. In spite of its hold upon society, and its uses and abuses of the past, the prison, as such, must go. The same religion which found its birth in man's weakness and degredation and brought forth the prison in the early morning of human experience, has decreed its extermination and that of every fetter that restrains human progress, even though many such fetters are its own offspring. This religion has been the curse and the blessing of the race and is destined to become its savior—the Religion of Humanity.

The prison first appeared in connection with the treatment of criminals in England as early as 1166, but it was not then a form of punishment. The Assizes of Clarendon provided a sort of " cage " in which to keep prisoners from the time of apprehension until trial, and after trial, if condemned, until execution. Punishment was still by fines, servitude, outlawry, or death. For the next six hundred years the horror of prisons is beyond description. Innocent individuals, arrested on false charges by malicious persons, were compelled to live for months in these squalid places with the very scum of the earth, the most hardened and depraved criminals, until the time of the next gaol delivery. Small, unsanitary, reeking with filth, the prisons were invariably overcrowded. In 1785 Newgate contained

600 persons; in 1801, 650; in 1802, 720. In 1813, 340 persons were confined in a place built for 100, and in the female ward, 120 occupied space inadequate for 60. Later 1200 persons were confined in a gaol covering three-fourths of an acre.[1] The clothing worn by the prisoners is described as ragged and filthy, and both it and the wearers went unwashed save when an individual was dragged beneath the pump in the yard by his fellows and soaked until the humor of the crowd was sated. At night each occupied a space eighteen inches wide and as long as his person, the floor being entirely covered in this fashion.

The prisons were originally communal and unrestricted freedom of communication was permitted among the prisoners—male and female. The prisoners' families were allowed to visit them during the day, and friends, including prostitutes and burglars, spent much of their time there. Fresh crimes were planned there and for the payment of a fee to the keeper the most desperate criminals were sometimes allowed to go forth to perpetrate them.

Solitary confinement was introduced by act of Parliament in 1778, but was long in being established. The new cells were 7 x 10 x 9 feet. When the " fury of innovation " led to the reformation of the prisons, education was suggested as a remedy for the cure of the criminal disposition and this fad was pushed to such an extent that the Reading Gaol became famous as " Read-Read-Reading ". This absurdity reached its height when the scriptures were made the sole object of study and were even committed to memory. Du Cane cites an instance of one culprit who grieved at his liberation because, as he said, " he had gotten only as far as Ephesians." He later reappeared for stealing sheep, " in order," as he said, " to learn the rest." [2]

[1] DuCane, *The Punishment and Prevention of Crime*, p. 41.
[2] *Op. cit.*, p. 57.

Strange to say, punishment by imprisonment originated outside of the prison. Workhouses were provided to keep idlers busy. Various devices such as cranks, tread-mills, and windlasses were installed for the inmates to operate as a punishment for idleness. In 1715 workhouses were made to do duty as prisons and thus imprisonment became a form of punishment.

Under this system, gaolers became rich from fees extorted from their charges and men bought and sold the office of keeper of the prison like any other business. In 1561, such an office was sold for 5000 pounds, and the income from some of the largest gaols sometimes amounted to 4000 pounds a year. The fees consisted of charges for fire, brooms, candles, *etc.* Prisoners were ironed so heavily to extort money that it was difficult for them to move or to sleep. Others were chained to rings in the floor or compelled to lie with heavy bars across their legs. Finally the right to keep the gaols was bought by the crown for 10,500 pounds. This put an end to the nefarious barter of the privileges. Gradually the solitary confinement system was adopted until at present, in all our modern prisons with the exception of county jails, the cellular system is well-nigh universal. The work-house feature has survived in our immense penitentiaries which are often large manufacturing plants. The fee system was long retained. It survived in New Jersey until 1906, at which time some keepers were making as high as from $7,000 to $30,000 per year by speculating in prison supplies. This abuse was finally abolished at the instigation of the " *New Jersey Review of Charities and Corrections* " and a salary was substituted for fees by law.[1]

The motive for imprisonment at the present time is three-

---

[1] Allen, *Efficient Democracy*, ch. i.

fold. The idea of punishment still survives and consists of loss of liberty and forced labor. The reformation, at least of a part of the prisoners, is still strongly hoped for. The third idea, and the growing one, is the protection of society by the detention of the criminal, and to this highly-scientific motive, still clings the ancient deterrent idea.

The verdict of writers upon penology is almost unanimous in its condemnation of the existing prison system. Of this as a whole Drähms writes,

The prison, from every point of view, is the chief ostensible promoter of every ill it essays to cure, and offers the main incentive to crime in the objective and exemplary inducements it holds out thereto by virtue of its congregate system of indiscriminate herding together of all classes of offenders. Hence, it is safe to say, it succeeds in turning out more direct results in the shape of confirmed criminals, hardened to the contemplation of theoretic vice in all its forms and degrees, ready to put their knowledge into practice, than any other accredited agency within the range of experience or devised by the folly of man, resting on the consent of the masses.[1]

A striking case in point occurred on Randall's Island in the House of Refuge for Boys, February 13, 1908. Twenty boys armed with knives engaged in a pitched battle which resulted in the death of one and the serious injury of three others. The knives were stolen from the teachers' desks purposely for the occasion. The boy that was killed had been arrested about a year before and committed for grand larceny, having been an inmate of the Juvenile Asylum previous to that time. He was killed by his " pal " by accident.

Ellis notices the evil effects of short sentences upon both the incarcerated and society. " The prison indeed, as it

[1] *Op. cit.*, p. 193.

originated, is a sewer throwing out into society a continuous
flood of purulence, the germs of physiological and moral
contagion.   It poisons, brutalizes, depresses, corrupts.   It
is a manufactory at once of the phthisical, the insane, and
the criminal."   In the same vein Fredur writes:

Looking at our present system of dealing with thieves, examin-
ing it from every side, it is clear that nothing can be more
clumsy and inefficient—except for evil. Let any one of robust
health fancy himself a prisoner within four walls, employed
day after day in the severest labor, without a face to look at
except that of a tyrant warder or of a scrowling criminal,
without relaxation or kindly intercourse of any kind; with
nothing, in short, to subdue the darker feelings, but with
everything to nourish them. Let any one of robust health
fancy himself doing this year after year for a fifth, a fourth,
or even half a life, and then say what sort of a creature he
would probably become. Then there is the expense of a
system which does not reform or get rid of a thief—in old
days gaol fever did the latter when the halter failed—it merely
hordes him up for awhile to turn him loose upon society more
wolfish than ever. As we deal with the thief he is our most
costly national luxury.[1]

The fate of the wrongly-imprisoned person is practically
sealed when the prison doors close behind him.   Numerous boys, sentenced because an exuberance of energy has
led them to the violation of petty ordinances, graduate from
the jail, fully equipped and trained for a criminal career.
Only in isolated cases is reformation effected.   The remarkable success of certain efforts made to provide work
and respectful treatment for discharged prisoners only veri-
fies the same fact as is demonstrated by Judge Lindsey's
special treatment of juveniles, namely, that a large number

---

[1] *Sketches from Shady Places*, pp. 206-7.

of offenders ought never to have been imprisoned in the first place. The truly marvelous thing about the matter is that many are not made criminals even by incarceration. Allen cites the following instances to show the awful results of unjust punishment:

A small boy of nine is in an ill-ventilated, dark room in a county gaol. For what? He is accused of having stolen a pair of shoes worth $1.25. He has already waited for trial 53 days, at a cost to the county in board alone of $13.25. He must still wait 30 days, although his gaolers are convinced of his innocence.

In a nearby county gaol is a young woman *décollettée*. For ten weeks she has been attended only by male gaolers, at an expense to the county of 50 cents a day for board alone. She herself is charged with no offense, but is waiting until her state finds three men who drugged and assaulted her while she was returning from a party. The state does not pretend to be looking for the men.

A girl of seventeen, of somewhat more refined features than the other women about her, confesses that she is serving her second sentence. She is willing to do anything but go to a reformatory, or to take any steps that suggest a desire on her part to regain her footing. Further inquiry established the fact that until her first sentence she had been a good girl. Her mother in a fit of temper made a complaint of disorderly conduct, that is, pounding on a door and screaming. During her 90 days in gaol, associations and habits were cultivated that required her return soon after discharge and made of her a confirmed criminal.[1]

In the case of the true criminal, the loss of liberty is compensated by the guarantee of three meals a day and comfortable quarters; and, after one incarceration has cleared

---

[1] *Op. cit.,* p. 186 *et seq.*

his mind of notions of the terrors of prison life, the prisoner looks upon detention merely as one of the chances of
business. The only hardship is the requirement of hard
labor, which is rarely inflicted except for felonies. This
permits a vast number of criminals to enjoy seasons of rest
and recuperation at the expense of the state. With such
astonishing regularity do many avail themselves of it that
McDonald suggests that the parting word of the released
prisoner to his less fortunate fellows be " *au revoir,*" not
" *adieu.*"

The following performance is so often repeated that it
becomes monotonous, to both the court and the accused.
The prisoner is released from custody at the expiration of
his sentence; he plunders society; the machinery of the law
is set to work to catch him and bring him to trial; the state
then hires lawyers to defend him as well as to prosecute
him and, after his conviction, remands him to prison
again; at the expiration of a period more or less determined
by law, during which he has been kept and nourished at
the public expense, the state is compelled to release him and
the whole performance begins again. The victims of this
process are well described by McDonald as roving parasites
which society is unable to shake off.

The luxurious accomodations and considerate treatment
accorded to criminals in many prisons are higher than the
standard of living of hosts of honest working men, and
present a continuous temptation to the shiftless and those
averse to toil. When conditions become such that the
comforts of the prison tempt honest but worsted citizens
to become malefactors, the menace to society, bad enough
at best, becomes many times multiplied. It is a well-known
fact that numerous persons of low moral sensibilities spend
their summers at odd jobs, petty thieving, and " hoboeing "
about the country, and, at the first approach of cold

weather, get themselves committed to assure warmth and comfort through the winter at the expense of the state. Such an instance came to my notice in a Jersey court last winter. A well-known character had just been sentenced by the judge to 30 days in the county jail, more to get him off the hands of the community than anything else. After sentence had been pronounced, the good-natured judge said, " Well, Charlie, what do you think about it?" After a suggestive shiver which shook his miserable rags, he replied, " It's pretty cold, Judge." Whereupon the sentence was made 60 days instead of 30.

McKim cites the case of a Parisian scamp, who, wishing to be sent to prison to escape the necessity of providing for himself food and shelter, entered a large restaurant and there ordered and consumed a breakfast worth eighty francs. Afterwards he coolly announced his inability to pay. The proprietor, saying that he had no time to waste over the matter at court, simply had the man put out. Later, in a similar fashion, he obtained a meal at a hotel, and there too was unsuccessful in his effort to be arrested. Only after a third or fourth trial of this method did he succeed in getting himself incarcerated.[1]

The disastrous effect of short-term imprisonments is everywhere marked. A few quotations will suffice to show the strong terms in which the well-nigh universal custom is condemned. Dr. Drähms writes:

So long as chronic and hardened offenders are visited with short and easily-served sentences, so long will imprisonment have its fascinations, and incarceration prove conducive to the criminal habit. Statistics show that short sentences are a bid upon habitual law breaking and an incentive to the chronic repeater.[2]

[1] *Op. cit.*, p. 178.   [2] *Op. cit.*, p. 226.

If, as Dr. Drähms asserts, recidivism is accountable for the rapid increase of crime, and is itself on the increase, a most serious charge lies at the door of the penal system. The state prison, he continues, with its present methods of incarceration and the absurd systems of sentencing and punishing in vogue are the chief external agencies that go in aid of the recidivistic habit. Brevity of sentence in the case of the recidivist, and undue length of punishment in the instance of first offenders, tend unequivocally and irrevocably to create and infix the criminal temper, and induce almost certain repetition.

The disaster which results from the imprisonment of an innocent person or of the petty offender who is not a hardened criminal is presented in the following lines from Henderson: " Imprisonment even for one night is a serious penalty and injury, even if the person is set free at once. If a short penal sentence follows for a slight offense the prisoner is disgraced, he is registered with thieves, he is affected by their conversation, and is likely to enter into a criminal career."

On the other hand, the short sentence is just as disastrous when applied to the hardened criminal. On this point the same writer says: " The mere temporary caging of the criminal, as a wild beast, is a protection of society for the time being, it is true, but if when he is let out of his cage he is worse than he went in, more inhuman, more brutal, more bitterly disposed toward his fellows, he may be more wary and cunning thereafter, but he will be more dangerous to society than before he was caged."

The astonishing frequency with which the short sentence is pronounced is shown by Ferri, who quotes French statistics. We have reason to believe that the conditions are not much different in other countries. The total number condemned to imprisonment by the French tribunals, and detained by the police in the years 1879 to 1888 was 1,675,000; the tribunal sentences under six days being 113,000. The total condemned to punishments of various kinds by the assize courts, tribunals and police courts, reached in the same years the enormous number of 6,-440,000 persons. The meaning of this is that the penal system of the present moment is a vast machine, devouring and casting up again an enormous number of individuals, who lose amongst its wheels, their life, their honor, their moral sense, and their health, and fall into the ever-growing ranks of professional crime and recidivism, too often without hope of recovery.

Several absurdities of the system are pointed out by Allen in the following pointed sentences: " if these men are in gaol for the sake of protecting society or to better the men, neither effect is accomplished by permitting them to associate in idleness with confirmed offenders, learning to despise the name of justice, and to disdain, if not to hate, society. If they are imprisoned merely because they cannot pay fines or costs, then it is poor business to keep them idle, when they might be working and paying the fine." [1]

Much agitation and a vast amount of experiment must occur before the prison relinquishes its place in the treatment of the criminal, but go it must. At present it is generally conceded by those who have taken the time to consider the matter that the criminal by passion or accident, ought seldom to come within its walls. The same is largely true of the occasional offender. He is a harmless individual in the main, and there are other ways of treating his periodic or intermittent infractions far better suited to social protection. If, however, his outbursts are a menace to society, the same treatment should be accorded to him as to the born criminal. Insane and born criminals, the latter class in-

[1] *Op. cit.*, p. 188.

cluding habitual and professional criminals, will be restrained for life. Such being the case, how can the prison be dispensed with? Let us see.

The prison must go, but it will not be in a night. Its passing will be gradual, almost imperceptible; it is in process even now. First destined to perish is the lingering idea of punishment. Its accompanying idea of deterrent value is even now being prepared for interment. Would that we might bury them both in one grave. Next to follow will be the still hardy hope of reformation which is now building massive institutions and determining the shape of others to be built. Its demise is more remote but its ultimate abandonment is certain because of reasons already hinted at in the chapter on the death penalty, and which will be more fully stated in the chapter on propagation. One feature, however, whose germs have lain dormant from the very beginning, but which have recently sprung into life, is destined to survive and occupy the field alone— the idea of social protection. The sole surviving feature of the prison will be detention, but that, stripped of all its present impediments will no longer have the nature of imprisonment. Work will be necessary for the good of the detained and to reimburse the state; solitary confinement will be retained only for those individuals whose liberty would endanger the lives of their fellow exiles. In this ultimate institution, stripped of all its barbaric features, will be restrained all individuals whose natures have declared them unfit for social responsibility—an asylum for personalities whose response to environmental and social stimuli has been and bids fair to be criminal; an institution whose fundamental idea will no longer be expressed by the word prison.

CHAPTER VIII

THE JURY

ONE of the ideas of natural rights inherent in the Anglo-Saxon peoples is the idea that every man accused of crime, or injustice, which is never far removed from crime, has a right to be tried by his peers. While the jury in essence is not peculiarly an Anglo-Saxon idea, this deeply-grounded conviction in the minds of that people throws light upon the probable origin of it. In all probability it is the survival or outgrowth of the old tribal custom of trying all cases before the popular assembly composed of all the free men of the tribe. Spencer makes much of this custom. Tacitus gives us an interesting account of one of these tribal meetings. The men of the tribe all attended in response to some pre-arranged signal and sat in a group in the midst of which space was allowed for the speakers. The meeting was sometimes presided over by the greatest warrior or a revered elder, but this functionary had no authority to decide issues. Any person wishing to speak was permitted to do so, and agreement with his suggestions was expressed by the thunder of the short knives of the armed men upon their shields. Decisions were made by popular vote, although most punishments were established by tribal custom.[1] The appearance of the jury among the ancient Jews under the Mosaic laws, and in ancient Athens and Rome, instead of testifying to any other source

[1] *The Germania.*

of the jury, indicates only that these peoples were once tribally organized as were the Germans described by Tacitus, as Morgan has ably demonstrated.[1]   Whatever may have been the time or nature of its later introduction into England and, still later, the continent of Europe, the fact remains that it arose and developed as the effort of a people or rather a state or stage of society to meet conditions to which it was subjected.   Ferri points out that it has not met with favor among certain nations in Europe because it was introduced there and not developed.   He thinks it must finally disappear because of this fact.[2]   On the other hand, it will be long in disappearing from the English-speaking peoples because of its evolutionary nature among them.   But even now it has begun to pass, owing to numerous weaknesses in the fundamental idea in connection with present conditions.   The tribal conditions out of which it grew gave to it its efficiency.   These have long since ceased to exist.

This fundamental idea is that a man shall be tried by, or subjected to the judgment of a group of men, usually twelve in number, who are his peers, *i. e., like himself;* and, as long as society was in such a state that men could be found approximately alike in large numbers, no great difficulty presented itself; but with the breaking-up of strictly nationalized peoples and the wide spread of diversity among individuals, the difficulty of finding twelve men who are peers of the accused becomes correspondingly greater.   This resulted in the adaptation of the idea itself to the changed conditions and at present the practice rests upon the supposition that twelve men can be had on all occasions who are capable of *judging between error and truth.*   Shifted to this basis, it at once becomes evident that such a group

---

[1] *Ancient Society.*   [2] *Op. cit.,* p. 195.

of men can be got together only under the rarest circumstances and then with the greatest difficulty. What is
usually the case is a panel of individuals as widely diverse
as it is possible for twelve persons to be and each probably
holding a different conception of truth and error, if he is
sufficiently educated to have worked out for himself, or accepted, a definite position at all.

But granted that twelve such men are found ready to
hand when needed and are impaneled without successful
objection on the part of the claimant or prosecutor and the
the defense, there remains yet another assumption for the
attainment of justice, namely, that twelve men be impaneled of candid mind *without prejudice of any sort.*
Here it seems we have presumed the impossible under normal conditions. We believe it to be impossible, at the present time, for the average judge or sheriff to get together,
under ordinary conditions, twelve men, or a group con-
taining twelve men, who would be chosen for jurors who
could be said to be without bias of some sort which would
influence them for or against a claimant or prisoner regardless of the evidence presented in the course of the trial.
Mr. Spencer in his volume on the *Study of Sociology,*
notes some of the " biases " which in his time were to be
overcome before one could successfully study social science.
These were: 1, the educational bias; 2, the bias of patriotism; 3, the class bias; 4, the political bias; 5, the theological bias. Changing the phraseology somewhat, but re-
taining the ideas in each instance we have a summary of
the prejudices which would influence jurors to the detriment of justice, although unknown to themselves.

What Mr. Spencer calls the bias of patriotism we have
already considered under race prejudice, which must play
an important part where the prisoner happens to be of a
nationality different from that of an individual juror and

between whose respective nationalities a strong antipathy
exists. The class bias would be fatal to justice in a case
where a wide diversity of social standing existed between
the accused and his jurors; especially in a case where a man
of high social standing has the misfortune to be tried before
a jury of laborers who hold a marked prejudice against his
class because of social privileges enjoyed by him which are
beyond their reach. The political prejudice is not so
marked, but it is a force to be reckoned with. The religious bias must not be overlooked. Considering the bitter
animosity which still exists between Catholic and Protestant in certain western communities and even that which
occurs among rival Protestant denominations, we find a
most subtle hindrance to perfect justice when a diversity
of religious belief exists between the prisoner and his jury.
Broad-minded as the learned men of our great religious
bodies may be, the average juror is drawn from the great
mass of believers who hold an inherent aversion for unbelievers or the equally great mass of unbelievers who suspect
that the believer would wish them eternally damned. In
addition to these, relationships, though so remote as not to
constitute a legal barrier to jury service, past associations of
an intimate nature, personal convictions and ideas of justice
and morals which may be sincerely held by individuals and
yet be very different from the general ideas upon these subjects, all tend to render the juror unconsciously prejudiced
for or against an accused person and make the attainment
of justice improbable in proportion to the extent of that prejudice. Another great impediment of the jury is its susceptibility to emotional influence. Even in the most enlightened
and unprejudiced individuals it is impossible to eliminate entirely what is vulgarly called sentimentality, a susceptibility
to an appeal to the emotions. As a result of this many trials
are a sentimental fiasco in which the lawyers exert their

oratorical and magnetic powers to render the jury blind to true justice by the excitation of their emotions. On this point, Ferri writes:

The predominance of sentiment over the intelligence of the jury is revealed in the now incurable aspect of judicial discussions. There is no need and no use for legal and sociological studies and for technical knowledge; the only need is for oratorical persuasiveness and sentimental declamations. Thus we have heard an advocate telling a jury that " in trials into which passion enters, we must decide with passion." Hence, also, the deterioration of science in the Assize Courts, and its faulty application, and its completely erroneous consequences.[1]

The tremendous influence of public sentiment, even though maudlin, upon jurors frequently prevents the attainment of justice and many times the decision of the jury is only the opinion of one man on that jury, who, by reason of his personality and persuasive powers, has been able to bring his eleven colleagues around to his way of thinking. This condition leads Ferri to conclude:

The verdict of the jury cannot represent the sum of spontaneous and individual convictions—not only in countries where juries are exposed to all kinds of influences during the adjournment of the discussion, but even in England, where unanimity is required, and where all communication of the jury with the outside world is forbidden until the end of the trial. For in every case the influence of the most intriguing or most respected jurymen in the jury's room is always inevitable.[2]

When the dominant individual or group of individuals is susceptible to bribery or personal interest the precarious situation of justice is evident. The same writer also notices

---

[1] *Op. cit.*, p. 192.   [2] *Ibid.*

" the inevitable tendency of the jury to be dominated by isolated facts with no other guide than sentiment, which, especially in southern races, confines all pity to the criminals, whilst the crime and its victims are all but forgotten. The very keenness of sentiment which would urge the people to administer ' summary justice ' on the criminal when surpised in the act, turns entirely in his favor when he is brought up at the assizes, with downcast mien, several months after the crime." [1]

One of the many absurdities of criminal law demands that the juror render his verdict without consideration of the result of such a verdict upon the accused, a psychological impossibility which is recognized in some localities where capital punishment is practiced in the fact that jurors who have conscientious scruples against putting a prisoner to death are not permitted to sit in murder trials.

We now come to the consideration of Mr. Spencer's first bias—that of education. Probably the average American juror is the most intelligent juror in the world, yet it is no reflection upon him to say he is wanting in the technical knowledge requisite to a satisfactory performance of his duty. Even apart from technical notions,

which we consider necessary to the physio-psychological trial of an accused person, says Ferri, social justice certainly cannot be dispensed through the momentary and unconsidered impressions of a casual juryman. If a criminal trial consisted of the simple declaration that a particular action was good or bad, no doubt the moral consciousness of the individual would be sufficient; but since it is a question of the value of evidence and the examination of objective and subjective facts, moral consciousness does not suffice, and everything should be submitted to the critical exercise of the intellect. [2]

[1] *Op. cit.*, pp. 191-2.				[2] *Op. cit.*, p. 185.

In addition to this he notices " a fatal defect, which alone is sufficient to condemn this institution of the law."

In the first place, it is not easy to understand how a dozen jurymen, selected at hazard, can actually represent *the popular conscience,* which indeed frequently protests against their decisions. In any case, the fundamental conception of the jury is that the mere fact of its belonging to the people gives it the right to judge; and as the ancient assemblies are no longer possible, the essence of the jury is that *chance alone* must decide the practical exercise of this prerogative.[1]

The idea of the fitness of this " casual juryman " to deal with one of our most important social problems is directly opposed to the principle which dominates present-day economic conditions. For instance, " no one would dream of having his watch mended by a cobbler," or of having an ignorant longshoreman arrange the intricate legal details of a valuable estate. In conclusion, Ferri advances his " two inevitable arguments of human psychology."

First, the assembling of several individuals of typical capacity never affords a guarantee of collective capacity, for in psychology a meeting of individuals is far from being equivalent to the aggregate of their qualities. As in chemistry the combination of two gases may give us a liquid, so in psychology the assembling of individuals of good sense may give us a body void of good sense. This is a phenomenon of psychological fermentation, by which individual dispositions, the least good and wise, that is the most numerous and effective, dominate the better ones, as the rule dominates the exceptions. This explains the ancient saying, " The senators are good men, but the Senate is a mischievous animal." . . . Secondly, the jury, even when composed of persons of average capacity,

[1] *Op. cit.,* pp. 186-7.

will never be able in its judicial function to follow the best
rules of intellectual evolution.   Human intelligence, in fact,
both individual and collective, displays these three phases of
progressive development: common sense, reason, and science,
which are not essentially different but which differ greatly in
the degree of their complexity.   Now it is evident that a
gathering of individuals of average capacity, but not technical
capacity, will in its decisions only be able to follow the rules
of common sense, or at most, by way of exception, the rules
of reason—that is, of their common mental habits, more or
less directed by a certain natural capacity.   But the higher
rules of science, which are still indispensable for a judgment
so difficult as that which bears on crime and criminals, will
always be unknown to it.[1]

We have yet one assumption to deal with, which may lay
claim to being the most fundamental assumption of the
whole jury system, namely, the assumption that guilt or
innocence can be determined by testimony.   This discussion
involves us in a consideration of two of the greatest defects
in the whole system, the unsatisfactory nature of testimony
because of diversity of impressions and the inability of
witnesses to tell what they have seen and heard in a manner
to convey the true situation to the understanding of the
jurors.   One or two examples will be sufficient to illustrate
our statement.   Mr. Parmelee, in his splendid chapter on
Evidence, gives the following interesting quotations.[2]   The
first is from *Archives de l'anthropologie criminelle,* for
March, 1906.   At a trial in Germany three witnesses, an architect, a teacher and an elevator man, testified each as follows as to how they went down together in an elevator; the
architect, that all were standing up, the teacher, that he sat

[1] *Op. cit.,* pp. 188-9.
[2] *Anthropology and Sociology in Relation to Criminal Procedure.*

and the others stood, the elevator man, that he stood and the others sat. In this case, two, and possibly all three, were not telling the truth, and yet it is highly improbable that any one of them was wilfully misrepresenting the facts. The second incident is most interesting. At a meeting of the " Association of Legal Psychology and Psychiatry of the Grand-duchy of Hesse," at Göttingen, during one of the sessions, a clown and a negro rushed in and, after an excited altercation, rushed out. Each person in the audience, for whom this occurrence was quite unexpected, was asked to write an account of it. Forty reports were handed in and of these there was only one whose omissions of important details amounted to less than 20 per cent. Fourteen omitted 20 to 40 per cent of the important details, twelve omitted 40 to 50 per cent, and thirteen more than 50 per cent. There were only six that did not make absolute misstatements of facts; in twenty-four reports 10 per cent of the statements were manufactured, and in ten more than 10 per cent of the statements were absolutely false.[1] Mr. Parmelee suggests that an expert in psychology be appointed to examine each witness before testimony in order to ascertain his value as a witness. Would not this procedure be just as advisable in the case of jurors?

In spite of the importance of such objections to the jury as have already been given, there remains to be stated the principal reason for its abandonment. In the treatment of crime, in the light of the conclusions already arrived at in this book, there are three matters of paramount importance. The first is to ascertain the exact nature of the crime and the circumstances and conditions connected with it. This information is to be obtained by the appointed agents of the state and should all be obtained before the supposed

---

[1] L. W. Weber, in *Beitrage zur Psychologie der Aussage*, vol. iv.

criminal is brought to trial. The second is to ascertain whether or not the accused actually committed the crime. The third is the matter of determining the nature of the criminal, after it has been shown that he is such, and the means best adapted to protect society from him in the future. This makes evident the fact that the services of the jury are needed, if at all, in the second consideration—that of determining whether or not the man on trial committed the crime in question. Even if the jury be retained to determine this fact, the beneficent results of such a method are evident even to the most superficial observer. Among the most gratifying results would be the removal of the necessity of the attempt to prove a complicated charge against the prisoner because the nature or extent of his punishment would no longer be determined by the nature or extent of his crime. The results of this would be far-reaching. Many rogues whose guilt is potent escape punishment because of technicalities which unscrupulous lawyers are not slow to avail themselves of. In a strict legal sense the prisoner is not guilty if it can be shown that a single detail of the charge is not correct. The state has the privilege of a new trial on a new charge but after two or three costly attempts at justice have been made the prospects of conviction become remote and the case is thrown out of court. In this manner the most influential and wealthy malefactors, who are often the greatest criminals, escape the demands of justice while the less powerful and poorer persons, though not nearly so dangerous to society, suffer the extreme penalty of the law. It is feared at present that too many of our greatest commercial enterprises are carried on by criminal methods, but captains of finance suspected of criminal acts proceed practically unmolested because of the remoteness of the possibility of bringing them to judgment.

An immense amount of legal jugglery would be eliminated and the " shyster " lawyer would be driven from the practice of criminal law if the only function of the jury were to determine guilt or innocence. The question to be answered by the jury would be, " did the prisoner commit the act in question?" This change would eliminate pleading and sentiment from the trial and remove one of the greatest hindrances to the attainment of justice. Mercy would no longer enter into the consideration because the nature of the punishment would not be determined by the jury's verdict. The question of blame or guilt would no longer be involved since punishment would have ceased to be retribution and would have become simply social protection.

The true question involved is whether the man on trial is or is not a menace to the safety and peace of society. If such, he should be restrained, if not, he should be restored to society. The crime is merely an indication of the true nature of the person committing it and not an index of punishment to be inflicted upon him.

Owing to the importance of this decision, because of its determining what shall constitute one a menace to society, or better, what persons are a menace to society, the jury should not be composed of twelve chance persons but a group of experts, trained in criminal anthropology and sociology and psychology. They should be maintained by the state for this particular function. Thus the second and third divisions of criminal procedure would fall into one and the whole of a criminal case would receive consideration at the hands of experts instead of being subjected to the blundering ignorance of an ever so honest and well-meaning populace. This body would combine the information obtained in securing the conviction with the other evidences of the nature of the criminal derived from an anthropological and sociological investigation and the extent of a man's menace to society would be obtained. On the basis of this information it would then decide the best method of procedure in the matter of disposal of the prisoner and the settlement of the case in connection with him.

With the jury the office of judge would pass away also, in its capacity to determine punishment. What should happen is that the judge should become a juror, and the jury, a group of judges.

CHAPTER IX

Justice and Restitution

THE most consistent thing about the human intellect may be said to be its utter inconsistency. Equipped with the relative, it goes forth to explore the absolute and finds—its self. This realization of its self is the highest achievement of the human mind. Roving for ages in what it supposed was a boundless realm, it presently discovers apparently insurmountable barriers to its further progress. Being possessed of an inherent craving to know, it raises the question, Why? At this point in its existence it manifests its compound nature. The philosophic intellect, proceeding by the long, swift strides of logic, soon arrives at the unknowable, where it itself breaks up into two camps, the one portion, being unable to worship, is in despair; the other bows down in adoration. Science, on the other hand, is not concerned with the unknowable, but occupies itself with pushing back the boundaries of the unknown, and, since happiness springs from hopeful endeavor, offers its followers an opportunity to drink from a fountain of everlasting joy.

Figuratively speaking, the average individual intellect puts out its hand and receives from the darkness a bundle of wands by which it measures all the incidents of its experience. In this bundle, among others, are Time, Truth, and Justice. Balked by the difficulty of analyzing these, the human mind expresses them by personification. Thus Time is a swift creature, Truth a naked goddess, Chastity a virgin, Wisdom an owl, wide-eyed and silent, and Justice is blind. The wisdom of this portrayal is born of necessity, for we can never know the things in themselves. The individuals personifying them offer the easier task of stating all we know about them, which constitutes all the knowledge obtainable of the things personified.

By the average intellect these wands are accepted without question, but when some more inquiring person attempts an analysis of them, to his consternation they vanish like the mirage. Terrified by this manifestation of unreality he turns and grapples with material things to save his reason and is astonished to find the magic wands once more in his possession. This analysis, though beset with many dangers, is the road by which the individual progresses to Paradise. Once entered upon it, his personal worth determines his destiny. After his horror at the discovery of the chimerical nature of such terms has passed away, one of two things takes place. Either he frees himself from hard and fast mandates he has supposed to have been God-given and perishes in a hell of his own creation, or finds his soul's salvation in the realization of the infinite possibilities of Humanity.

Let us explore the darkness out of which the wands have come. Far back in the dawn of sentient existence, the wise law of survival presented a passport to unlimited progress to that creature which first manifested and then developed the love of offspring. Rising out of this love came self-denial and sense of duty, first to the offspring and then to its kind. From this developed, by slow degrees, the acknowledgment of the needs and wants of others which later become rights with their implied justice. Thus justice is born of pressure or restraint. If there had never been any restraint it is probable the idea of justice would never have arisen. The unrestrained expression of self in response to stimuli does not contain the germs of justice; not until this response is modified by consideration of some other than one's self could justice have existence. Out of the conception of the rights of others grows the conception of right conduct which includes the rights of all.

We have now arrived at the only statement of the meaning of justice which is thoroughly consistent and expresses the thing itself. Justice, in its very essence, governs conduct and the ideal justice is that conception which demands on the part of the individual such conduct as will not infringe upon the rights of others.

Current and accepted definitions of justice express this in a round-about way. They shape themselves into two propositions, the conception of equality and the idea of recompense. The confusion of these has been responsible for many of the vagaries of so-called justice in the past. As Mr. Spencer very definitely points out, the idea has been evolved, and the divers expressions of justice have been but the picture of the conception at that particular stage of its development, though, no doubt, many persons still believe that justice and its sister conception, truth, have existed the same in and for all ages.

This conception of justice includes the two-fold statement given above. Let no individual hope to escape the demands of justice by refraining from conduct of any sort, for, where the rights of others demand action, refraining from that action constitutes a wrong. If that action is demanded by the welfare of the state, refraining from it constitutes a crime just as wrong action does. Thus recompense is but the demand for action of some sort, and as long as the action is not forthcoming, justice, in that particular case, cannot be said to exist.

The difficulty of defining rights has been and is now the cause of much injustice. It has raised up advocates in the field of government ranging from the aristocratic absolutist to the anarchist, each asserting that his particular method would best serve justice in protecting the real rights of man. We have not time to quarrel with either extreme as to the method of conserving human rights, but it is most necessary to our discussion that we define these rights.

What are the real interests of the individual? Were he alone upon a tropical island the question would answer itself. His rights would be equivalent to his desires, and, since opposition to them would be reduced to zero, the rights themselves would increase to infinity, and would, in reality, be no rights at all. Thus it is evident that rights are a condition of social experience. The question of right, then, does not originate until the result of activity is felt by some other than the person acting, and wrong originates at the same time. One cannot exist without the other; were there no wrongs possible there could be no rights.

Let us now introduce a second individual upon our island and analyze conduct in the light of the new arrangement. The freedom of action of the first individual is now limited to the field of action which in no way interferes with the second, and *vice versa*. This field then becomes the field of right action and all action outside of it is wrong. Increase your number of individuals and the field of individual freedom grows smaller and a new factor appears in your arrangement. That which limits the field of action of the individual is no longer the rights of another single individual but the collective rights of a group of individuals, all of whom are subjected to the same restraints. A recent French writer expresses this relation in the following sentence: " Whatever has been, in fact, the origin of society, it has for its end . . . the protection of all the natural liberties, that is to say, all those forms of human activity which do not infringe upon the liberties of others." [1]   Thus

[1] Dugast, *La Justice Sociale.*

we have the only true justice in social justice, and in the last analysis, wrong action of any sort becomes crime. Sin, a matter of the individual, passes over into crime, a matter of society, in just the same proportion as the activity of the individual becomes an ever more and more important matter of the state. The closer and more compact the social bonds, the more important to the state becomes the activity of the individuals composing it.

During its development, justice has been involved with one of the most potent factors in human experience, namely, vengeance, whose union with religion produced a most vigorous offspring—retribution. Born of a union of two fundamental instincts retribution combined in itself the powers of its parents, and though destined to pass away it still stands between society and true justice. While vengeance may have sunk below the surface in some of our advanced societies, it has not yet gone to so great a depth as to be indiscernible in the limpid waters of human nature. " Nemesis, the goddess of vengeance, is gone," says Ross, " and in her place stands Justice, with bandaged eyes, holding the scales. But as we gaze longer, the figure melts away and there looms in the background the colossal Phantom of Society, with eyes wide open and the sword of self-defense in her hand." [1]

With the stolid characteristics of its parents to maintain it, retribution still occupies the field to a considerable extent. In the minds of many it fills the place of justice. Because of its very nature it oversteps the bounds of justice and is cruelly unjust. Growing out of repressive measures, it still resorts to repression. In its early history it was little more than vengeance. The whole history of its career is pictured in the history of a single people. First we are

[1] *Social Control,* p. 108.

introduced to a jealous God, who destroys not only individuals, but whole peoples with their innocent women and
children because of the slightest disobedience or on account
of his chosen people. Thus is deeply engrounded the idea of
retribution, the payment of a penalty, which idea still holds
a dominant place in the common mind. Among the same
people appeared the most noble God the human mind has
ever conceived of, whose only emotion at the waywardness
of his people is sorrow for their iniquity, and a divine
longing for their redemption. The same flesh and blood
which in its infancy wrote " I, thy God, am a jealous God,"
survived long enough as a people to catch a glimpse of the
kingdom of Heaven where " Thou shalt love thy neigh-
bor as thyself." Out of retribution has grown punishment.
out of justice grow sympathy and fraternity.

Justice concerns itself with all human action, a fact
which, as we have seen, grows more apparent as the inter-
gration of society proceeds. We must limit ourselves at
present to the consideration of one phase of it only, namely,
justice in the matter of crime.

By the very nature of social justice, the state is not permitted any privileges which are denied to its people as a
whole. It, least of all, can afford to be unjust; but in spite
of this fact, criminal justice, so-called, is the most farcical
activity indulged in by modern civilization. In the name of
justice society wreaks vengeance in the form of punishment
upon a criminal for a wrong done to one of its members.
This in fact is merely meting retribution to the offender
without doing justice either to the offender or to society.
True justice gives what is deserved both to the offender
and the offended. By deserved we mean that justice be
done to repair an injustice. Not that a certain form of unjust action merits a punishment, but that it necessitates a
re-establishment of justice. In the minds of thinkers there

is a growing doubt as to the offender's deserving anything
more than restraint for action which is but the natural
result of his constitution.   The retention of punishment
for social satisfaction is but a thinly-veiled form of vengeance and it does not satisfy justice in the least particular.
Some of the vagaries of the present criminal law are so
great as to be humorous were they not so absurd and such
a reproach to an enlightened people.   This condition leads
Allen to observe that " criminal equity has shaded penal-
ties according to fluctuations in the market rate of crime
with the grotesque precision ridiculed recently by an observer indignant at a sentence of 20 years and 17 days—
' I could account for the 20 years alright, if the judge would
explain how he got the 17 days.' "   The same author
cites the case of a girl of sixteen who was sentenced to two
years in prison for having stolen 50 cents; a woman of
forty was given two years for having " converted," to quote
the district attorney, " brunettes into peroxide blondes and
confined them in a brothel." [1]

The cause of this absurdity is not far to seek.   Punishment has been regulated by law, in the hope of prevention, according to the varying degrees of responsibility.
While science and reason have about concluded that responsibility is a conception instead of a condition, the punishments remain without their original foundation.   The
assumption that the criminal is such by deliberate choice
and therefore merits a corresponding punishment is rapidly
passing away and the growing tendency is to believe that
he merits nothing but commiseration, certainly not cruelty.
By the abandonment of retribution society can lose nothing because by it nothing was gained.   In addition to its
uselessness it stands in the way of reformation which is

[1] *Efficient Democracy*, pp. 185 *et seq.*

capable of rendering society a service while rendering
justice to both the injured and the condemned. Society
needs not that its criminals be punished, but that it be
effectually protected from them. Instead of revenging
itself for past wrongs it needs to protect itself from wrongs
in the future, which at present it not only does not do, but
by its efforts to gain revenge, it, in a measure, guarantees
an ever-increasing amount of future injury by hardening
the natural criminal and strengthening the purpose of the
faltering juvenile delinquent.

Present justice stops before true justice begins. We might
go further and say that, aside from the incidental protection of society during the time of the criminal's actual incarceration, no benefits whatever accrue from our present
criminal procedure. Even this incidental benefit is far
offset by the derogatory effects of the system upon the
prisoner and a general lack of confidence in institutions on
the part of the masses. Laws, to be successful, must in-
spire respect for law in general. So far are our present
criminal laws from doing this that instead or respect they
incur suspicion on the part of the ignorant and disgust on
the part of the enlightened, with a general lack of serious
respect in all between.

When all has been said and done, in the average criminal
trial at the present time, either one of two conditions exists:
either the accused is declared guilty and the demands of the
law are complied with, or his innocence is established and
his honor vindicated. In neither case is justice done. In
paragraph ten of the second chapter of *Civil Government,*
Locke gives the following analysis of the idea of justice.
While his conception of how a man becomes a criminal is
the accepted theory of his time, his idea of true justice is
far ahead of his period. We wonder how so clear a conception could have made so little impression. He says:

Besides the crime which consists in the violating of the law, and varying from the right rule of reason, whereby a man so far becomes a degenerate, and declares himself to quit the principles of human nature, and to be a noxious creature, there is commonly injury done to some person or other, and *some other man* receives damage by his transgression: in which case, he who hath received any damage, has, *besides* the right of punishment common to him with other men, a particular right to *seek reparation from him that has done it:* and any other person, who finds it just, may also join with him that is injured, and assist him in recovering from the offender *so much as may make satisfaction* for the harm that he has suffered.[1]

Here the robust plant of vengeance and the slender stalk of true justice grow side by side.

Nowhere in the history of organic development has the right to punish been demonstrated. Such a right is an assumption on the part of the person or persons holding that opinion. The right to reparation is everywhere demonstrated. In organic life the entire organism contributes to the repair of the injured portion. In society the whole group is vitally concerned in the welfare of the individuals composing it. In the past, almost the whole attention of law-makers has been given to determining and imposing a requisite amount of punishment upon the offender, while, until recent years, comparatively nothing has been done to redress the wrongs of the offended. True justice consists not in punishing the wrong-doer but in redressing the wrongs committed by him. The popular demands for justice are satisfied as soon as the culprit has been brought to judgment, but justice still cries out from the lips of the widows and orphans he has made, or the innocence he has betrayed, or from those who have suffered material loss or personal injury at his hands. Her voice is not stilled until resti-

---

[1] Italics are mine.

tution has been made as fully as possible to the injured
parties.

As soon as this conclusion is arrived at we are face to face
with the problem as to how redress shall be accomplished.
The problem is by no means easy of solution. It is a very
evident fact that in some cases the wrong done cannot be
repaired, as, for instance, a murdered father cannot be
restored to his weeping wife and children or virtue returned
to the unmarried mother or ruined virgin. But even in these
extreme cases approximate justice can be done. The question of immediate interest is, by whom shall this restitution or reparation be made? In most cases, the answer is
not far to seek—by the criminal himself. In a large
majority of cases, for the greater part of crime is petty,
the culprit can be made to restore the pilfered goods or
render their equivalent in money, not to the state, but to the
person injured. The fact that he has no means nor any
property to assess makes no difference whatever. Readjustment should be made by the state and the state should
exact the amount from the culprit by forced labor.

When, for any reason, the culprit is unable to make
restitution, or is unable to reimburse the state by his labor
for having made it for him, the duty of the state to make it
still remains. Society having produced the criminal, is responsible for his actions. When, by repressive measures,
society has not been able to protect one part of its consti-
tuents from the depredations of another, it becomes its
duty both to the injured and to itself to make good the
injury. Society has followed out the inconsistent course
of refusing to let the injured redress his wrongs personally
while refusing to redress them itself. This inactivity on
the part of society must eventually be as demoralizing to
social solidarity as would the free exercise of personal vengeance now prohibited by social restraint.

The individuals composing society gladly give of their substance, and, if need be, their lives to the maintenance of the government in return for which they receive a guarantee of personal safety and the security of their interests and liberties. Any failure on the part of the individuals to do this is punished by the state in the interests of individuals composing it. For the same reason, whenever the state has been unable to fulfil its part of the contract, it should make restitution for the damage resulting from its inability to perform its duties.

Thus for two reasons society is obliged to establish justice by the reparation of damages, namely, because it has produced the criminal, and because it has failed to afford its members protection against him.

It is evident at once, in the case where the accused is declared innocent, that all that has been said above still holds true. The actual wrong has been done and the victims of it are suffering just as much as they would be had the prisoner been declared guilty. The fact that justice has been done to the accused in the maintenance of his innocence establishes only one thing in regard to the real injustice, namely, that the real offender is still at large and a menace to society. The state is now under a double obligation to its members. The first is to indemnify the injured to the extent of its ability and the second is to secure its members against further injury at the hands of the culprit still at large.

But in addition to these there remains a third obligation, which is as insistent as the others or even more so. A cruel injustice has been done to the accused in many cases far exceeding in magnitude the injury of the offense with which he has been charged. Concerning this much has been said and little done. The right to protection from unjust prosecution, or remuneration for privation and loss, not to mention cost of defense, in vindication of one's innocence

is second only to that of the right to protection from loss at
the hands of malefactors. No one questions the duty of
the state in the matter of the one: why is not the state under
the same obligation in the case of the other?

An attempt to meet this obligation and a tacit acknowledgment of it appear in the custom of the appointment of
a defender by the judge at the expense of the state for those
persons brought to trial without council and who are unable
to pay for his services. The superficial nature of this practice is shown by Mr. Parmelee who discusses its numerous
weaknesses. The defense thus appointed is usually some
hanger-on of the court who is unable, through lack of
ability or experience, to obtain more remunerative practice,
and consequently not capable in many instances of defending his client properly in opposition to the clever prosecuting
attorney who wears laurels in proportion to the number of
convictions he is able to secure. In many instances, the lawyer thus appointed first ascertains whether his client is
able to pay a fee larger than that appropriated by the state
and in case he is not, urges a plea of guilty because such
procedure requires the least effort on his part to obtain the
pittance awarded for his services. This results in a false
plea of guilty on the part of many innocent persons who
consider it the shortest and most economical means of escaping from an unfortunate situation. The consequent penalty, whether great or small, produces either a hardened
criminal, ready for any offense, or a man embittered against
the injustice of the system of which he has been the unfortunate victim. To avoid this Mr. Parmelee suggests a
public defender with skill equal to that of the prosecutor,
with whom he should exchange duties occasionally.[1] The
value of such a suggestion is apparent in that its adoption

---

[1] *Op. cit.*

would guarantee all accused persons a fairer trial, but the injustice of the wrongful accusation still remains.

The friends of the present system defend it upon the ground that the state must have the right to accuse and prosecute in the interest of justice, and that the liability to accusation is one of the sacrifices each individual composing the state must make in order to conserve the public good. However no average citizen can be expected to be so patriotic as to become a willing martyr when nothing comprehensible to him is to be obtained or conserved by his martyrdom. In addition to this, his obligations to the state have been performed when he has placed a portion of his means and his person at the disposal of the state to avoid the necessity of just such a sacrifice. This fact entitles him to remuneration for all reasonable loss and privation which come to him as the result of the mistakes of the appointed institutions supported by him in conjunction with his fellows.

Remedial steps suggested by several foreign writers have been taken in this direction by various countries by enactment of laws authorizing the indemnification of unjustly imprisoned or punished persons, whose innocence has been established after a part or all of their sentence has been served. E. Ferri even advocates restitution to persons prosecuted through " malice or negligence." The writer would go further and state that the right to indemnification should not be denied to any person wrongly accused, and that the difficulty of determining such persons would disappear with the legal establishment of the right. The magnanimity of an enlightened people would guarantee that funds should never be lacking for the establishment of true justice, once a prospect of obtaining it were assured.

As Ferri suggests, the indemnification of persons wrongly imprisoned is already forcing itself upon the peo-

ple of Europe where scholarship and science walk on intimate terms with the department of justice. The progress of
such reform will cease only when true justice is satisfied by
the indemnification by the state of all wrong of this nature

The prospects of obtaining such justice as is conceived
of in this chapter are bright. Its claims are such that they
have only to be brought to the attention of an enlightened
people to be accepted. The principal delay will be caused by
the difficulty of adjustment, for institutions born of customs
linger long after their usefulness and the ideas which have
produced them have passed away. The substitution must be
a gradual one, but it has begun even now. Laws looking
to such reforms have been adopted in Portugal (1884),
Switzerland (1886), Denmark (1888), Austria (1892),
Belgium (1894), France (1895), Germany (1898 and
1904), and in many other countries. May we hope for it
such a characteristic as has been granted to so many of our
modern reforms—that of acceleration with progress.

Once established, true justice would guarantee, as nearly
as is possible with the aid of human instrumentalities, such
action as would conserve the rights of all, including the
state, those injured by the crime, and the accused, be he a
criminal or an innocent man.

CHAPTER X

Propagation

THE characteristic inconsistency of the human race mentioned in the beginning of the last chapter is nowhere more evident than in the attitude of the state toward the perpetuation of life. The most elaborate care has been and is being taken in breeding animals and producing new vegetable varieties while little in comparison has been done to improve the human race or even maintain it at its present standard. The departments of agriculture of the United States and of the various states annually expend large sums of money for the improvement of strains of cattle, horses, sheep, hogs, turkeys, chickens, *etc.,* while the quality of the *genus homo* is little considered. Occasionally a voice is raised in protest but it is drowned by the popular applause of a government so magnanimous. Not that what our government is doing in this line should not be done, but that the other ought not to be left undone.

Were the sin of omission the only one to be laid at our door in respect to propagation of the race our guilt would not be so great, but in addition to utter neglect of the matter of race perpetuation there exists our blundering methods of dealing with our delinquent, defective and dependent classes which not only permit such classes to exist and propagate, but often assist and encourage them to do so. If the same amount of funds were devoted to this subject annually as are given to the improvement of our domestic animals our criminal problem might be practically solved in the lifetime of the present generation.

No doubt much of our present condition can be accounted for by the religious ideas of the sanctity of human life which have prevailed and prevail largely at the present time, but with the present trend of religion towards humanitarianism and the high intellectual status of our citizenship it is time the wilful production of a child doomed before its birth to insanity, imbecility, or disease should be placed upon the catalog of crimes parallel with arson and manslaughter.

The present indifference of our legislators upon this subject is inexcusable in the light of our many well-known scientific discoveries. While many of the costly experiments now being made to rehabilitate our social wreckage will have to be carried out, the fact is none the less evident that rehabilitation, even if possible, should not extend to an opportunity for reproduction. " The correctional discipline which is sought for in our prisons and reformatories, although a necessary public duty, is vastly more expensive and unsatisfactory than the application of preventive measures would be." [1]

Lax laws governing marriage make it possible in almost any state for the most vicious, degenerate and afflicted to marry, and, in many cases, they have been encouraged to do so. Many persons are urged to marry in the hope that domestic life may lessen the probability of future criminality. Frequently inducements are offered to get paupers off of the hands of the state in this manner. Such short-sightedness constitutes one of the greatest menaces to our racial solidarity. While in many cases the immediate end is accomplished, the ultimate result is an increased amount of degenerate criminals and paupers demanding consideration of the next generation. Short acquaintances, begun in dance halls, bar-rooms or in the streets, parks, or public resorts, lead to immediate marriages which cannot result in anything but turmoil as soon as the desires of the moment are satisfied. When not terminated by divorce, desertion or actual crime, such marriages

---

[1] Harris, in an introduction to *The Jukes*.

guarantee a long period of troubled domesticity in the atmosphere of which numerous poorly-bred and poorly-fed children grow up to careers of crime or debauchery. Harris asserts that habitual criminals spring almost exclusively from degraded stocks and that their youth is usually spent amid degrading surroundings of physical and social defilement, so that only a flicker of the redeeming influence of virtuous aspiration is ever possible. The career of offenders so trained becomes a reckless warfare against society. By the time the officers of justice overtake them and consign them to prison, the habits of vicious thought and criminal action have acquired the strength and quality of instincts.

The question of criminal reproduction is a grave one. We have already cited facts to show the immense number of criminals who are born of criminal parents. The following from Maudsley gives one a further idea of the gravity of the situation:

All persons who have made criminals their study, recognize a distinct class of beings, who herd together in our large cities in a thieves' quarter, giving themselves up to intemperance, rioting and debauchery, without regard to marriage ties or the bars of consanguinity, and propagating a criminal population of degenerate beings. For it is furthermore a matter of observation that this criminal class constitutes a degenerate or morbid variety of mankind, marked by peculiar low physical and mental characteristics. They are, it has been said, as distinctly marked off from the honest and well-bred operatives as " black-faced sheep are from other breeds," so that an experienced detective or prison official could pick them out from any promiscuous assembly at church or market. Their family likewise betrays them as follows "by the hand of nature marked, quoted and signed to do a deed of shame." [1]

[1] *Op. cit.*

These types are familiar to our truant officers and are seldom improved by reformatory methods; they are the despair of the probation officers and children's courts. According to Drähms 50 per cent of the population of our industrial schools are either orphans or the children of divorced parents. " Divorce and crime go hand in hand and juvenile crime is sheltered beneath its wings." Of the 4838 juvenile male population in French reformatories in 1896, 4321, or 89.3 per cent, were illegitimate. Of the 1095 girls, 849, or 77.53 per cent, were illegitimate.[1] Respecting a majority of the Elmira criminals it appears that their intelligence is amply sufficient to account for apparent reformation, but for a true reformation their moral endowment is utterly inadequate. Says Herbert Spencer: " Creeds pasted upon the mind, good principles learned by rote, lessons in right and wrong, will not eradicate vicious propensities; though people in spite of their experience as parents and citizens persist in hoping they will." Still more—even when the pseudo-reformation lasts through life, the former criminal generally bears with him a capacity to perpetuate the vicious stock from which he has usually sprung. McKim quotes the following from an article in the *Arena* by Martha Louise Clark:

Since my experience as a teacher of imbeciles began, twenty of my boys have gone out to work for themselves. Fitted by their education to do some work well under patient direction they are still, as far as I know, for the greater part of the time inmates of the infirmaries, working for a while, then, as one of them told me, " resting." Of course, an occasional child makes a moderate success of life but only an occasional one. The great majority are sooner or later to become public burdens, usually after they have married an equal or inferior in

[1] *Statistique pénitentiarie pour l'année* 1896, Tableau vi.

intellect and brought into the world children who are a shade less desirable to the community than the parents.[1]

From the borderland of the defective and dependent a high proportion of our criminals are drafted annually. It constitutes a wide realm, as described by Maudsley, between the normal and the insane, and contributes of its degenerate population to all classes of criminals as shown by the following figure:

Fig. 7.

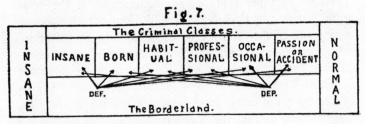

Although one of the first to write upon this important question Maudsley has given us a most admirable description of the process of mental degeneration:

It is a fact that a pathological evolution, or more correctly a pathological degeneration, of mind does take place through generations. The course of events may be represented as something in this wise: in the first generations we perhaps observe only a predominance of the nervous temperament, irritability, a tendency to cerebral congestion, with passionate and violent outbreaks; in the second generation there is an aggravation of the morbid tendencies, displaying itself in cerebral hemorrhages, idiopathic affections of the brain, and in the appearance of such neuroses as epilepsy, hysteria, and hypochondria; in the third generation, if no check has been opposed to the downward course, we meet with instinctive tendencies of a bad nature exhibiting themselves in eccentric, disorderly

[1] *Arena*, X, 790.

and dangerous acts, and with attacks of some form of mental derangement; and, finally, in the fourth generation, matters going from bad to worse, we meet with deafmutism, imbecility and idiocy, with sterility, the terminus of the pathological decline being reached. Such is the course of degeneration when it proceeds unchecked.

The unfortunate element in this process is that nature does not take steps to protect the race until so much damage has been done.

In the first three stages of degeneration the individuals are often most prolific, and, restrained by no moral sense, they flood the community with a numerous progeny one degree more debased and dangerous than themselves. Their illegitimate offspring is legion. The havoc is made worse when occasionally a robust and healthy individual marries into such a degenerate stock. The result here is only to delay the ultimate sterility two or three generations. This merely gives a larger opportunity for disastrous propagation—an opportunity which is not neglected.

The size of some of these families is phenomenal. Dugdale's study of the Jukes and McCulloch's *Tribe of Ishmael* give striking examples of their prolific natures. The latter contains a chart from a record including thirty families out of a possible 250 and covering a period of four generations. The individuals thus traced amounted to over 5000 interwoven by descent and marriage. " They underrun society like devil-grass. Pick up one and the whole 5000 would be drawn up." An investigation of this chart reveals numerous families producing six children; eight had seven; eight had eight; four had nine; one had ten; one, eleven; one, thirteen; one, fourteen; one, fifteen; one, seventeen, and one, twenty-two.

The dangerous inhabitants of this borderland are addicted to the use of stimulants of all kinds, thus showing their close relation to their criminal brethren. Of these stimulants alcohol in some form is the most common. So frequently do criminals of this class start their careers of crime while under its debasing influence that many students of the subject have been led to assert that a vast majority of crimes are the direct result of alcoholism. True it is, as Maudsley says, that "the vices of drunkenness, indolence, vagabondage, and prostitution lead directly to overt acts of an anti-social nature. The vices produce the crime, and there is no distinct line of demarcation between them." But are not the vices and crimes also parallel evidence of defective constitutions which, in the case of drunkenness, are allowed to express their true traits unhindered by such moral restraints as are possessed by the inebriate when sober?

Dr. McKim gives the following admirable definition of a drunkard: "the habitual drunkard is an individual who in obedience to a morbid instinct charges himself with a spirit of perversity and turbulence and returns to the society of his fellows as an explosive which any trifle may ignite into the most destructive violence." The following is one of a number of like histories given by Dr. McKim to show the awful effects of alcoholism upon the progeny of the inebriate. In the first generation the father was a drunkard. In the second generation an inebriate son was disgustingly drunk on his wedding day. In the third generation there were seven grandchildren. The first and second of these died of convulsions. The third was an idiot at 22 years of age. The fourth suffered from melancholia and suicidal tendencies and became demented. The fifth was peculiar and irritable, and the sixth was repeatedly insane. The seventh was nervous and depressed and indulged in most despairing anticipations as to his life and reason.

Entirely lost to shame and all sense of responsibility, the drunkard is as prone as the imbecile to multiply his kind. The temperate man may feel responsibility as to the rearing of his offspring. Not so the drunkard—he casts all that care upon the state which must reverently receive the life sprung from a source so foul, for by society human life is esteemed sacred and inviolable. Society may remonstrate but until caged or exterminated the drunkard is master of the situation.[1]

Thirty years ago, Maudsley felt compelled to say a word on behalf of the inhabitants of this unhappy region because of the inconsistency of the law which ascribed like powers of resistance to all and punished on the basis of moral responsibility. There is a borderland, he writes,

between crime and insanity, near one boundary of which we meet with something of madness, but more of sin, and near the other boundary something of sin but more of madness. A just estimate of the moral responsibility of the unhappy people inhabiting this borderland will surely not be made until we get rid of the metaphysical measure of responsibility as well as of the theological notion that vices and crimes are due to instigation of the devil and proceed by way of observation and induction to sound generalizations concerning the origin of the moral sentiments, the laws of their development, and the causes, course and varieties of moral degeneracy.[2]

The disastrous results of propagation among neurotic stocks has been demonstrated by Echeverria, who, after ten years' careful research into the character of the offspring of epileptics, published valuable statistics bearing upon the question. Excluding all cases not fully verifiable, he found that 62 male and 74 female epileptics produced 553

[1] McKim, *op. cit.*, p. 154.   [2] *Op. cit.*, p. 34.

children. Of these latter 32 were still-born; 195 died during infancy from spasms; 78 lived as epileptics; 18, as idiots; 39, as paralytics; 45 were hysterical; 6 had chorea; 11 were insane, and 7 had strabismus; 27 died young from other causes than nervous diseases. Thus out of 553 children 448 died early, or were very gravely afflicted, while only 105, or less than a quarter of the whole number, were healthy. Who will believe for a moment that the children of the 105 so-called "healthy" persons of this unhappy group can hope to escape their awful heritage?

The law of consciousness of kind works to a remarkable extent among the people of this unhappy region. How familiar to almost every community is its popularly-called "queer couple," whose union of peculiarities, either physical or neurotic, has almost invariably produced an equally "queer" offspring. Frequently such unions are childless. Because inheritance from defective parents on both sides produces a high percentage of neurotic children, this attraction of defectives and degenerates for their kind is, on first thought, alarming. On second thought, however, such attraction is seen to be merciful in that it reduces by 100 per cent, roughly speaking, the possibility of contamination of healthy stocks and by 50 per cent the possibility of neurotic children. This attraction is particularly strong among neurotics and was noticed by Maudsley as an "unfortunate circumstance" because of his belief that the neurotic tendency was minimized by marriage into a robust family.

Among paupers and the semi-dependent classes, as well as among criminals the working of this consciousness of kind is greatly intensified because of the lack of opportunity as well as inclination to marry outside of their own kind. The so-called law of aspiration works with increasing intensity the higher the social status; consequently members of the class immediately above those in question turn with repugnance from those they feel to be their inferiors. The pauper and criminal classes escape sterility and extermination only by the constant dropping down to them of the weaklings and degenerates from the numerous classes above, where the struggle for existence works with ever-increasing intensity.

Persons of talent and culture hover on the brink of this great social chasm but are inevitably dragged into it because of the greater weight of degeneracy and physical defect. For this reason the common or rather uncommon tramp has filled an interesting place in our popular literature which leads its readers to believe that the tramp is a wronged and abused victim of misfortune. The varieties of tramps range from roving workmen, often of exceptional ability, to shiftless and irresponsible vagrants. Of them as a class, Henderson writes: " the tramp is a vagrant beggar, in whom the roving disposition which characterizes defective natures is highly developed. He is a modern Bedouin. The tramp is a distinct social peril. He carries vermin and loathsome contagious diseases from place to place. In his person and habits syphilis finds a nidus. He communicates his disposition and disease to his children. He is a constant iniquitous menace to life and property. He is a venal voter in dense communities, and a corrupting element in politics." " Tramps," says McCook, " constitute a great part of the force of chronic offenders and drunkards who march in procession before city police judges and receive short sentences. Free soup houses only increase the plague. Work must ever accompany relief. Any remedy which helps tramps at the expense of the industrious poor, as by taking work away from the sober to give it to the drunkard, cannot fail to hurt society." [1]

[1] *Charities Review*, June, '92.

Dr. Giddings, while emphasizing the necessity of educating the children of parents who cannot or will not care for them, at the same time holds that it is one of the duties of society to " enslave—not literally but physically—all those men and women who voluntarily betake themselves to a life of vagabondage. The time has passed when food and shelter should be given by kindly sentimentalists to the tramp, or when the public should deal with his case in any partial way. Every tramp within the borders of civilization should be placed under arrest and put at severe, enforced labor under public direction." [1]

Thus we get an idea of the motley characters which inhabit the borderland. We have described only a few, but their number is legion. Miserable, ignorant, afflicted, degenerate, they have ever furnished a ready outlet to maudlin sentiment and fanatical religious altruism, unscientific and irrational in the extreme. Nor has the state been innocent of this pseudo-altruism. Numerous almshouses have set a premium upon idleness and shiftlessness and afforded unbounded opportunity for illegitimacy and crime. Fortunately their day is passing, although they linger, a vile pollution to the heart of many communities.

Very much of the altruism of the church has been of this irrational type. Washington Gladden, in an article on " The Municipal Church," says,

One bane of church charity is its indiscriminate, emotional, unreasoning, unscientific almsgiving. Its benevolence is often malefficient rather than beneficent. Sectarian almsgiving, a sort of ecclesiastical (I refuse to say religious) bribery, is to blame for the pauperization of many a family in our cities. Missions vie with each other for the opportunity of destroying the self-respect and self-help of poor families, by distributing

[1] *Democracy and Empire,* pp. 95-6.

old clothes and fitful supplies of groceries, while they refuse persistently to co-operate through the association of charities in wise measures for exterminating the cursed disease of pauperism.

Of this same tendency, McKim writes, in his characteristically vigorous manner: " in these days the hopelessly weak are received as a special charge from heaven and to the sad detriment of their more promising brothers a double portion of wealth and affection is lavished upon them; while of the criminal it is hardly an exaggeration to say that he is regarded as a being whom society must reform though ninety and nine just persons thereby severely suffer." The present indiscriminate distribution of food by several lower East Side missions is a typical expression of this popular tendency. The managers of the " bread lines " seek to defend them by means of the testimonies of their beneficiaries, a proceeding as illogical as the bread line itself. All such indiscriminate efforts only increase the miserable conditions of the slums, so well described by Drähms:

There are no homes here, properly speaking, only places of temporary shelter and promiscuous herding, the sole conditions under which thousands of our city's lowest classes subsist, and where they raise their progeny in utter disregard of the decencies and moralities of life, oftentimes glad to be rid of their responsibilities by means fair or foul. These are the raw material that makes roughs and desperadoes, and city toughs, cast in the moulds of an implacable environment as cruel as the grasp of necessitarian law. Ninety per cent of the acquired criminalism of the land is thus begotten and raised in, and receives the initial stamp of, the social environment in which it is engendered and which holds it ever after true to its ideal. As rapidly as the young produced in this seething caldron of immorality fall into the hands of the state we spare no pains to preserve them alive and make them as dangerous as possible by our efforts at reformation.[1]

Of the feeble-minded alone who are received and trained in institutions, ten to twenty per cent, according to Henderson, are so improved as to be able to re-enter society as bread-winners; from thirty to forty per cent are returned to their families so improved as to be self-helpful, or at least, much less burdensome to their people; and further, and of greater importance, one-half the whole number will need custodial care so long as they live.[2] But what of this other half? Restored in body and sufficiently improved in mind to guarantee their maintenance, its members are sent out into society to marry and multiply, thus increasing their kind and bringing a taint into every healthy family they enter. The present effort to redeem the waifs thrown upon the shores of this veritable " slough of despond " is like trying to stem the flow of a river by damming it at its mouth. The task is an endless one as long as the fountain flows.

The idea that poverty, disease and crime are due in any large measure to accidental or unfortunate circumstances is no longer tenable. Men as a rule find their level as surely as water does. Every reader will be able to call to mind instances of misfortune or accident, but these exceptions only prove the rule. McCulloch, in the conclusion of his study of the *Tribe of Ishmael,* asks, " What can we do?" He then suggests three things. First, close up official relief; second, check private and indiscriminate benevolence or charity, falsely so-called; third, get hold of the children. To these we would add a fourth: above all we must stop

---

[1] *Op. cit.,* 284.

[2] Henderson, *Def. Dep. and Del.,* p. 96.

reproduction on the part of all defective, dependent or criminal persons who fall into the hands of the state and prohibit by law the marriage of all persons physically or mentally deficient or afflicted with inheritable diseases. This can and must ultimately be done. The right to marriage and to offspring ceases to exist when marriage or offspring become a menace to society. Contrary ideas of rights are deeply grounded in the people, but we have no warrant for them. Fully grant to good and bad alike the right to live, to enjoy all the pleasures of life possible to them, but the right to procreate must be denied to those who, by their nature or conditions, can but increase their own misery, and that of their fellows, and subsequent generations. If among the multitude of popular conceptions of rights we admit the justice of any, certainly one of these is the right of every child to be well born. It becomes more and more the duty of the law to see that this right shall not be violated.

CHAPTER XI

A Remedy

EXTRA-LOGICAL imitation, says Gabriel Tarde, is divided into two parts, which he calls custom imitation and fashion imitation. The former constitutes the larger part of the great mass of human activity and is, for the most part, an unconscious repetition of, or imitation of, the activity of the past. The latter, a much smaller but none the less important part, constitutes all action in imitation of the new. Thus we have thinking humanity divided into two camps—the one cherishing the things that are because they are largely the things that have been, the other aspiring to the new and zealous for its claims and possibilities. Each is necessarily antagonistic to the other, for at the same time that the new threatens the extermination of the old, the old strives to throttle the new at its birth. Strange to say, out of this one-sided struggle, progress comes. By sheer force of genius, the few who recognize the superiority of the new over the old are able slowly to draw the great mass of worshipers of the past from a lower to a higher level of human existence. Some few ultra-conservatives refuse to respond, even to this upward calling, and are ostracized or ignored by society as fanatics; others speed in advance of the most progressive and are hanged as anarchists or revolutionists, or tolerated as harmless fools.

Lombroso accounts for this state of affairs by saying that all men are by nature either conservative or progressive. The one who by his nature responds to the appeal of the past or of the present falls into the conservative ranks and

finds his happiness in admiring its grandeur and expound-
ing its perfections and, if he be of belligerent temperament,
in defending it from the attacks of its mortal enemies, the
advocates of the new. He who, in like manner, responds
to the appeal of the new, finds himself in the ranks of the
progressives, and, while recognizing the many excellencies
of the present and the past out of which it has grown,
presses eagerly forward toward the infinite possibilities of
the future. The resultant controversy entails criticism and
publicity out of which the discerning mind comprehends
truth. The weapon of the conservative is usually the wrath
of God, that of the progressive is criticism.

Unfortunately for the cause of progress, many small
minds are dragged, by sheer force of the upward calling,
out of the comfortable grooves of their ancient highways
and, unable to progress further, amuse themselves by shattering the cherished ideals of their erstwhile brethren. The
destructive critic is a true iconoclast and deserves nothing
at the hands of society but a speedy extermination. The
true criticism is constructive and substitutes for the idol it
shatters a more adorable God. The destructive critic has
no excuse for his existence and no aim in life but to cause
discomfort and suffering; the constructive critic destroys
only to substitute the better way with the good of all in
view.

The advocate of progress, then, saves the best of the old
alive, if that be possible, but where all possible remedies
would leave the old still thoroughly bad, there is no course
open to him but to tolerate it until something better can be
had to take its place. There is only one condition under
which destruction of the old is permissible and that is where
it is removed to make place for the new. Even there outright destruction is impossible without a corresponding
shock to society. The substitution of the new for the old

must be made without interfering with the work of the institution.

Our criticism, then, of existing conditions in criminal
procedure and general methods and practices, is not for the
purpose of destroying the old wantonly but that the substitution of the new may be made possible before disaster from
ignorance and inadequate methods overtakes our social system. The daily loss of life, property and means, resulting
from present methods, ought to be sufficient to bring even
the most obstinate around to the view that radical change
of some sort is badly needed.

The very scientific discoveries which have accounted for
the inefficiency and disasters of the present systems unmistakably point to and trace the lines of the new institutions
which must ultimately replace them. As we have stated
elsewhere, men will doubt the compass and costly experiments will be tried because of mistaken interpretations of
the signs of the times; but in spite of this we believe the
ultimate solution of the criminal problem will be more or
less definitely along the lines suggested in this chapter.

It is a defensive system, to borrow the words of Ferri,
which, in the nature of things, must of necessity be substituted for the criminal and penitentiary systems of the classical school. As soon as the daily experience of every nation shall have established the conviction that these systems
are incompatible with the needs of society, so soon will it
be adopted.

We have endeavored to maintain the position that the
death penalty is not a practicable solution of the problem
from humane standards. Disastrous as the humane sentiment has been for the race in one direction, it has untold
value for it in another. We can hope to mitigate its bad
results without destroying its beneficial influence only by

abandoning such a method of readjustment. Speaking of
the practice of capital punishment, Dr. Drähms writes:

Does the average homicide commit his offence with the fear
of the law before his eyes? From a purely psychological
standpoint, *does he stop and think of the consequences of his
deed?* [1] Manifestly not. . . . It is a question of expe-
diency that requires the test of time and experience for its
solution so far as effective deterrence is concerned, while as
to its purely mediaeval features, it (capital punishment) might
well be dispensed with in favor of a more civilized substitute. [2]

This substitute we offer as a part of our system of social
protection.

We have given many reasons why the prison system
should be abandoned. It might safely be said that it fails
in all it essays to accomplish. It does not protect society
or reform the criminal; on the other hand, it is a school of
crime and a menace to our social institutions. With the
passing of the idea of responsibility and retributive justice
its very *raison d'être* has passed away. For a like reason,
the jury no longer answers a definite purpose, but tends to
assume judicial functions without judicial capacity.

Thus the removal of the very foundation of these institutions necessitates the reconstruction of our whole system
of criminal procedure, a fact which is keenly appreciated
by all scientific investigators. Substitutes or remedies are
offered more or less definitely by Lombroso, Ferri, Garofallo
and others of the Italian school, as well as Tarde, Ellis,
Drähms, McKim, Allen and others. While most of their
suggestions are in the nature of remedial changes, we feel
that the alteration of the present system must be in the form
of steps toward an ultimate substitution of an entirely dif-

---

[1] *Italics mine.*   [2] *Op. cit.,* p. 361.

ferent one. The main question is not how can our old systems be repaired, but how can society be most effectively protected with the least cost to itself and the least cruelty to the criminal.

A means of so doing is not far to seek; it has been suggested in part by several writers, most notably by Ferri, of the Italian school, and Dr. Drähms in America. It is nothing more nor less than segregation, permanent detention after identification, for the best interests, both of the criminal and of society. The idea of punishment should be eliminated, the prisoner should be kept in all the reasonable comforts of life until his death from natural causes. He should not be confined as a retribution for crime he has committed, but because he has shown himself a menace to society. In this segregated existence he should be compelled to work to reimburse the state for the expense of his maintenance and also as far as possible to repair the damage done by his crime if he has not had the means to make this reparation before his incarceration. Upon his entrance into the segregated state he should be considered as legally dead and should lose all rights and privileges as a citizen. His property should devolve to the next of kin according to law in the usual way in case of death. Of this system Ferri writes:

First, care must be taken that segregation does not come or continue to be (as it too often is at present) a welcome refuge of idleness and criminal association instead of a deprivation. Penitentiaries for condemned prisoners—the classical prison experts make no distinction between their cells for prisoners before trial and those for convicts—should not be so comfortable as to excite the envy (a vast injustice and imprudence) of the honest and ill-fed rural laborer, vegetating in his cottage, or of the working man, pining in his garret.

Secondly, the obligation to labor should be imperative for all who are in prison, except in case of sickness. Prisoners should pay the state, not as now for their tobacco and wine, but for food, clothes and lodging, whilst the remainder of their earnings should go to indemify their victims.[1]

The assurance that a definite number of hours of work per day would be required, without hope of escape or liberation till death, would be a sufficient restraint and prevent any shiftless or irresponsible citizen from deliberately choosing to enter into confinement to escape the responsibilities of life.

This system is already in practice in some localities with regard to the insane criminals. Born and habitual criminals also should be segregated as soon as identified. No pardon should be possible except in case of error in commitment.

The professional criminal would disappear as a class if detention and capture meant permanent removal. The chances would be too heavy against success and the profession would be abandoned.

The occasional criminal should be treated scientifically, in keeping with the tendencies manifested. A tremendous proportion of crime is committed by him. If the nature of the crime is such as to show that the culprit is a permanent menace to society, he should be removed promptly. If his occasional delinquencies show him to be a confirmed petty criminal, he might be allowed his liberty after steps had been taken to prevent his having progeny and after bondsmen have been secured to make good his occasional depredations. However, the wisest course would be his permanent removal from society. Recidivism once fully established would take him out of the occasional group and identify him with the insane, born or habitual classes. On

[1] *Crim. Social.*, p. 228.

this point Dr. Drähms writes, " Relapse is the distinguishing peculiarity of the genuine criminal everywhere. The natural instincts and predisposing bent of the congenital and habitual offenders are instinctively toward repeated transgressional acts as the legitimate outcome of his criminal propensity. With him, as has been truly said, reformation is the exception, recidivation the rule." [1]

The deterrent influence of such a system would be tremendous, far exceeding that of any present method of treatment and its principal influence would be felt at the period where it would accomplish the most. The hardened criminal would no longer be at large to act as school-master and idol for the still wavering juvenile; and the prison would no longer mean a place where, surrounded with comforts superior to those of his daily experience, the malefactor might plan for still more daring and thrilling adventures. The prison should be a place from which he should never return, once he entered.

An additional deterrent influence might be added, namely, the loss of franchise for a definite period, with restricted habitation, in addition to reparation for small offences not entailing segregation. By this means the offender would be compelled to live in a certain territory, from which he should not be allowed to move without having notified the authorities of his intention and also in regard to the place of his future residence. Removal from this specified district without such notification would constitute him a fugitive from justice, and he would be subject to arrest like a common criminal. " French leave " would be considered as a second offence. Ellis suggests that in dealing with occasional criminals, whom it is not necessary or desirable to put into prison, liability to imprisonment should be sub-

[1] *Op. cit.*, p. 222.

stituted. The system of recognizance and of fines to the community should be substituted and extended to all cases to which it may suitably be applied. When the offender is unable to pay a pecuniary fine he should not be imprisoned but compelled to work it out. Allen writes: " it is better for a man to support his family by work outside of prison than to make a public burden of them and himself while he attends a school of vice. If cash fines may safely be accepted in lieu of imprisonment, fines on the instalment plan should have even greater moral and economic value." [1]

The criminal by passion or accident should never be punished in any way or segregated unless the crime were clear evidence of social menace. In all cases of crime by passion or accident restitution should be made as completely as possible to the injured party. Where the offender is unable to do this he should bond himself to the state to reimburse it by labor for making it for him.

The International Prisons Congress of Paris, 1895, recognized " that the right to damages exists. That the injured party should have a lien upon the real estate, and a first lien upon the personal property of the guilty party."

Ferri would take from the penal code all crimes which we have classified as by passion or accident.

The object is to prune the long and increasing list of crimes, offences, and contraventions of all acts which result in slight injury, committed by occasional offenders, or ' pseudo criminals,'—that is by normal persons acting merely with negligence or impotence. In these cases the personal and social injury is not caused maliciously, and the agent is not dangerous, so that imprisonment is more than ever inappropriate, unjust, and even dangerous in its consequences. Deeds of this kind ought to be eliminated from the penal code, and to be regarded as

[1] *Efficient Democracy,* p. 192.

merely civil offences, as simple theft was by the Romans; for a strict indemnification will be for the authors of these deeds a more effectual and at the same time a less demoralizing and dangerous vindication of the law than the grotesque condemnation of a few days of imprisonment.[1]

It will be seen at once that the great problem involved in the application of this system is that of the identification of the criminal, *i. e.,* to determine the group in which he belongs. These groups have now reduced themselves to two. The one is composed of the insane, born, habitual, professional and some of the occasional criminals, the other, the remainder of the latter and criminals by passion or accident. Once it has been determined to which of these groups the criminal belongs, the problem in regard to his treatment has been solved. The following is a suggestive method which might be elaborated to fit almost any situation.

Many cases, by the very nature of them, will determine the class of the criminal at first offence, such as deliberate, premeditated murder, arson, wounding, *etc.* Ferri would include the latter crime among less serious offences. He believes that " in order to establish the fact of incorrigibility, the number of relapses should vary in regard to different criminals and crimes. Thus, for instance, in the case of murders, especially by born criminals, the first crime should lead to an order for imprisonment for life. In the case of less serious crimes, such as rape, theft, wounding, swindling, *etc.*, from two to four relapses should be necessary before the habitual criminal is sentenced to such imprisonment." [2] The number of offences necessary to segregation would thus, in a large measure, be due, not so much to the gravity of the offence as to the nature of the crimi-

---

[1] *Crim. Social,* p. 162.   [2] *Ibid.,* 252.

nal revealed by the crime. In this manner the offence
loses much of its importance for our present systems.

In all cases where the class of the prisoner is not determined by the first offence, or where he has been located in
the less serious group, full restitution of damages to the
injured party and to the state should be required. In a
large number of such cases the natures of the criminals
would be clearly revealed by the second offence and cause
them to be either segregated or recognized as occasional
criminals of a practically harmless nature. The remainder
of this group, however, whose identity could not be determined, should receive a multiplied penalty. In addition to
restitution, loss of franchise, as already described, should
add to the deterrent influence of restitution. To make this
still more formidable, restitution by money might be forbidden by the state for the second offence and the offender
compelled to make recompense by forced labor, though at
liberty.

Almost invariably the third offence would reveal the true
nature of the prisoner. He would be found to be either insane, or a born, or, what is practically the same thing, an
habitual criminal and, as a result, suffer segregation regardless of the nature of his offence. This progression in punishments was practiced by the Anglo-Saxons and also by the
ancient Germans. Among the Saxons a thief was fined for
the first offence. At the second offence the fine was doubled,
and at the third, still increased; at the fourth offence the
culprit was outlawed and his property confiscated by the
state. The outlaw was to be slain by any man on sight.[1]
It will be observed that under such a system the utmost importance would attach to the crime since principally by it is
the true nature of the criminal determined; the trial would

[1] Lee, *Source Book of English History*, Laws of King Edgar.

become an investigation of a medico-legal and psychological nature and preclude the possibility of the current farcical attempts to establish responsibility. If, says Ferri,

we rid ourselves of the assumption that we can measure the moral capacity of the accused the whole process of the criminal trial consists in the assemblage of facts, the discussion and the decision upon the evidence. For the classical school, on the other hand, such a trial has been regarded as a succession of guarantees for the individual against society, and by a sort of reaction against the methods of legal proof, has been made to turn upon private conviction, not to say the intuition, of the judge and court.[1]

If the ethical method of punishment as a retribution for crime be excluded from the repressive function of society, and if we regard this function simply as a defensive power acting under law, penal justice can no longer be squared with a minute complication of the moral responsibility or culpability of the criminal. It can have no other end than to prove, first, that the person under trial is the author of the crime, and then, to which type of criminals he belongs, and as a consequence, what degree of anti-social depravity and readaptability is indicated by his physical and mental qualities.[2]

The actual guilt, then, or innocence not sufficiently demonstrated by the expert investigation of the crime, might be determined by a jury of capable men, trained for this duty and appointed by examination. This should be the limit of their instrumentality in the proceedings. When the actual guilt of the prisoner has thus been established, responsibility to the state, *i. e.,* the disposal of the prisoner, is to be determined by a group of experts in sociology, criminal anthropology, psychology, physiology and medicine. The office of judge should be abolished for criminal cases, unless

[1] *Op. cit.*, p. 165.   [2] *Ibid.*, p. 163.

the judge be retained as a sort of moderator of proceedings. " In this case," says Ferri, " we shall have no more
of those combats of craft, manipulations, declamations, and
legal devices, which make every criminal trial a game of
chance, destroying public confidence in the administration
of justice, a sort of spider's web which catches flies and lets
the wasps escape." [1] Punishment will no longer be meted
out in proportion to the gravity of the offence or the degrees
of responsibility determined by an elaborate legal scheme,
but the prisoner will be handled reasonably in view of his
physical and mental condition and the demands of society.
In his conclusions upon the subject Ellis writes:

We still treat our prisoners with punishment and contempt.
And it has proved to be equally unreasonable, equally ineffective. The time is coming, has indeed actually come, to do
for the criminal what Tuke, Pinel and others did for the
insane. Hence the immense importance of Lombroso's identification of "moral insanity with instinctive criminality." The
social reaction against anti-social actions is a primitive and
inevitable fact of all social life. But it is in our power to
shape this inevitable social reaction. We may ameliorate
conditions that produce anti-social action; we may treat the
anti-social person in such a way that he may cease to be anti-
social. And in the last resort we can place him where he is
unable to gratify his anti-social instincts.[2]

" The plea for his (the criminal's) seclusion," writes
Drähms, " is one of social necessity. Society's claim is self-
defense. To eliminate what is dangerous sets the bounds.
To *punish* is beyond its prerogative under given conditions." [3]

[1] *Op. cit.*, 164.   [2] *The Criminal*, p. 367.
[3] *The Criminal*, p. 357.

The criminal is a product of society and, having produced him, society is bound to protect itself against him. Segregation is the only satisfactory and practical solution of the problem. Were Dr. McKim's remedy of extermination practicable it would be a speedy solution and an effective one, but by such a method the humanitarian instincts which have produced our degenerate classes would perish at their execution and the progress of the ages would be lost. Our altruism can be trained to expend its energies and develop itself in amelioration of human conditions at the same time that society by adopting segregation protects itself from harm. Thus can an artificial selective process be substituted by philanthropy for the natural one which was destroyed by it, and the development of humanity receive an added impulse at the same moment that a restraint is removed.

CHAPTER XII

EDUCATION

THE great instrumentality which produces advancement, like the mills of the gods, grinds slowly. Forgetful of this fact, many who would suddenly bring about social reforms lose patience with humanity and abandon it to its wrongs. Radical laws are forced upon the statute books by some sudden wave of feeling and later repealed or ignored because the strong sentiment which brought them into being no longer exists. By some persons their repeal or their unobservance is looked upon as a calamity, an indication of retrogression in social ideals. On the contrary the true state of affairs in such a case is that social ideals have not retrograded, they may have advanced even, but that an abnormal wave of social sentiment has subsided to the normal level, which may itself be rising. A few such experiences as this teach the observing the impossibility of forcing ideas upon society.

All laws, to be effectual, must be an expression of the will of the people. The real way, then, and the only successful one to bring about reform by legislation, is to bring about a *change in that will*. The world was not made in a day, nor was anything in it that was enduring. The quick to rise and blossom has ever been the quick to decay. Social advancement has been stable because it has been slow. Its progress was measured by cycles in the beginning and is still marked by centuries. In fact the greatest safeguard to society has been its tendency to make haste slowly. This has saved it from freak development and unstable conditions; without stability progress would never be. Reformers have mistaken this stability for indifference when, in reality, it is only aversion to change, especially change which is untried and doubtful. The reformer often urges new schemes because his inspired vision has caught a glimpse of the promised land, but the populace is still mindful of the leeks and onions of Egypt. Not until a whole new people is reared and educated for the new things can the actual change be made, long after the reformer has been cast out or crucified. When the whole group has advanced to the point of seeing his holy vision, his tomb is decked with garlands and monuments are raised to his memory.

Lombroso tells us that the anarchists commit their bloody deeds under the impression that the ideas they entertain are those of the masses and that once the tyrants are destroyed the whole populace will rise up and rejoice with them in liberty. Spies, only at his last hour, perceived that humanity is misoneistic, *i. e.,* a slave of habit, and he said, " to my great surprise I have had to learn that the great mass of men are followers of routine and call usage their nursing mother." [1] Revolutionists escape being rebels or anarchists only when the ideas they represent are held or espoused by a sufficient number of the population to make their efforts successful.

Dr. McKim affirms that gratification of his desires is the fundamental element of that mental tendency of man which we term selfishness, and that this we shall never eliminate. It is probably due to this that society is so slow to accept change unless the individuals composing it profit directly thereby. In the absence of this direct profit, change which is for the general improvement of social conditions is brought about only by enlightenment of the masses.

[1] *Les Applications de l'anthropologie criminelle,* p. 8.

It is a well demonstrated social fact that very few persons think for themselves. The individual consciousness is the last and best product of the whole of human development.[1] The great bulk of humanity thinks in families, groups, and masses. The independent thinker in politics and religion is rare. The great mass of voters and votaries vote and worship in accordance with the conditions into which they are born. They accept without question the common ideas of right, duty, justice, *etc.,* and are not roused by the most flagrant injustice if it conforms to their accepted code. Our present mockery of justice and the absurd legal labyrinth about the detection and conviction of criminals which lead to the most flagrant and absurd fiascos called trials seem not to have aroused any sentiment whatever in the breasts of the people. Occasionally a newspaper editorial calls attention to some gross miscarriage of justice but even this is forgotten in the craving for the sensational which is demanded even at the expense of the moral. The famous case of Captain Van Schaick and the burning of the General Slocum is a typical instance of the popular demand for justice. In this as in all other like cases the public was satisfied as soon as the regular routine had been gone through. Only by repetition of such crimes and repeated and persistent comment upon them can the defect in the laws thus revealed be enough felt by the people to bring about a remedial change.

But the cloud, no bigger than a man's hand, has already appeared over the sea in the matter of reform in criminal procedure. We almost hear the sound of abundance of rain. Of late, says Allen,

There has been a tendency to challenge the belief of our forefathers as to gaols and gaolers, judges and juries, and their

[1] Giddings, *Unpublished Lectures.*

remedy for crime. We talk less of vengeance and vindication of the law, deterrent effect of short hair, stripes and lock-step. In public, at least, penologists urge the humanity and the economy of reforming offenders, of preventing crime, turning on more light, training and educating criminals to correct distorted ideas. We now defend the indeterminate sentence that fits the man's need, not his crime. Everything is 'done to prepare the prisoner for his return to industry instead of emphasizing his isolation. To test the keeper's judgment that a man may be trusted he is paroled until a relapse is unlikely. But all our talk has not yet affected one per cent of the changes in criminal jurisprudence that our newer and humane professions demand.[1]

Great social reforms are brought about by one of two things—a vital need affecting the masses, or by enlightenment. In this case no need is felt, even remotely, by the people as yet, hence the necessity of education. It is the general opinion of those who make these conditions their study that every available means ought to be employed to acquaint the people with the actual situation and the menace of it. The St. Petersburg Congress recommended that, " in order to interest the public in penal and preventive questions, it is desirable that ministers of different religious bodies should coöperate in this work by devoting a Sunday to addressing their congregations in regard to prisoners." The secular press and popular lecturers and speakers should be induced to present the matter so that every citizen would have a knowledge of the entire field and he should be taught to see the place and relative importance of every effort made to improve conditions. " We are not," writes Henderson, " merely to medicate and dress an ever open sore of pauperism, insanity, idiocy, and crime, but to cure it." [2] People

---

[1] *Efficient Democracy*, p. 184.   [2] *Op. cit.*, p. 270.

need to know that " indiscriminate alms-giving is a distinct social peril," and toleration of law-breaking of any kind lays the foundation for social ruin. It is true that " large communities are not easily led to consider swiftly changing needs," but persistent presentation of those needs by a few consecrated souls will raise up a host of converts to uphold their arms when they fall from weariness.

The wisdom of such an educational procedure is manifested by the present wide-spread movement against the use of alcoholic beverages as a result in part of the introduction into the text-books of our public schools a generation ago of information upon the deleterious influence of alcohol upon the human organism. Much of the effort of the church has been wasted in the past by threatening inebriates with eternal damnation. Since the populace has been taught that indulgence in alcoholics is conducive to the destruction of body and mind, of family, and home, and happiness, concerted action has been brought to bear against it successfully. The tremendous part played by alcoholism in crime is now helping on the crusade. Ellis points out that "the danger of alcoholism from the present point of view, lies not in any mysterious prompting to crime which it gives, but the manner in which the poison lets loose the individual's natural or morbid impulses whatever these may be."

In spite of all our patriotism and pride of institutions we are compelled to admit that very little interest is taken in matters of state by the people. Matters religious are largely turned over to the clergy and politics to the political machine. To one we give our money and to the other we give our votes. We cannot hope for clean social conditions until personal interest be removed from politics. The one great need of our country to-day is patriots like unto those of '76—men, honest men, business men, who have love enough for our institutions to sacrifice their business interests enough to see that we get those clean governmental and business conditions which we have a right to expect. As long as decent men will not take a hand in politics from purely economic reasons, we can expect to be ruled by grafters and manipulators.

Efforts to educate the populace upon this somewhat gruesome subject will meet with no great encouragement from the people at first, on account of a deep-seated antipathy for crime and criminals in the popular mind. For ages past criminals have been looked upon as being possessed with devils or cursed of God. The idea that they are human beings and not much different from their fellows can only come from association or from giving a candid hearing to advocates of their cause. When we come to realize that they are what they are, not because of their desire to be so but because of their very nature, our loathing will give place to pity and our indifference to interest.

Much of our action in regard to our dependent, defective and criminal classes in the past has been characterized by ignorance and inefficiency. Our indifference is probably due to our inherent selfishness, as Dr. McKim says. A recent well-known writer, speaking of the almshouse in a newly formed American community, says:

During the first stages of its development it acts as a charitable catch-all for the community. Idiots, epileptics, incurables, incompetents, aged, abandoned and foundlings and a considerable number of the deaf and dumb and the insane are all dumped together in some old farm house that has been bought by the authorities and put to this use. The public then goes on its way and thinks as little about the institution as possible, only grumbling at the expenses, perhaps, when it happens to review the public accounts.[1]

[1] Quoted by McKim, *op. cit.*, p. 230.

In many counties, no longer to be classed as new communities, something like this condition exists. In the light of our present intelligence, such indifference on the part of the people is inexcusable. But, we are happy to say, in a great majority of our communities, we can point with pride to the scientific progress of our asylums for the aged and infirm, as well as for the idiot, imbecile, and insane. Our orphanages and charitable institutions speak well for the progress of humanitarian sentiment amongst us, while our system of free education has warded off many an impending disaster by softening and curbing those inherent savage instincts which are not very far submerged beneath our intellectual depths.

It is necessary for us to take but one step further to the scientific and sympathetic treatment of society's other children—the criminals. When once this step has been taken we shall be astonished to find how the solution of this, our greatest social problem, has thrown light upon other social difficulties. With the segregation of our criminal classes and the disfranchisement of our dependents and defectives, the greatest incentive to corruption in politics and the administration of the law will have been removed. One great difficulty in the way of such a change lies in the utter inconsistency which appears in our laws governing crime. In order to escape from these inconsistencies, honest and conscientious judges give themselves the widest latitude in the interpretation of the law, but, as Ellis writes, it is not by shuffling evasion of law that civilization progresses. We need just and reasonable laws, not merciful judges or juries.

If scientific study of man and society has shown us that the criminal situation is not met by our outgrown institutions, why continue our present ludicrous spectacle of developing clever manipulators whose sole business it is to make black appear white and vice, virtue? The following from the New York City police commissioner's annual report is brutally frank but pertinent:

Too many lawyers live by showing people how to break the law safely. Much of our modern legislation is ineffective because it is subjected in execution to out of date precedents and technical tricks. Why else does the liquor dealer cheerfully produce bail, confident that a chemical analysis will be required of his whisky?

How else in Sunday theatres is a dance not a dance, nor a costume not a costume, nor a play not a play?

How else is it that a racing bet is not a racing bet?

Is it not common sense that when the police cannot openly and in uniform buy tickets to a boxing bout it is because there is to be a prize fight?

Is it not common sense that gamblers have no need to fortify themselves unless they intend to break the law?

Refusal of admittance to the police in these cases is evidence of guilt, and we all know it.

Is it common sense that a policeman does not know the taste of whisky sufficiently well, at least for purposes of evidence? Why to get a definition of whisky that will satisfy the courts is now a national joke.

Do we propose to do anything about all this or are we all " in the same boat " ?

No, we are not " all in the same boat," but our selfish indifference to the situation places us dangerously near it. Our attitude gives a semblance of truth to the remark of a warden of a western penitentiary recently. " If a man steals a ride on a railroad we call him a hobo, if he steals the whole railroad his name is emblazoned in history as a financier." One of our well-known district attorneys is reported as excusing himself for throwing dice for drinks and money by saying that citizens of high character and great intelligence and distinguished position do such things; that

they also play cards for stakes and that " such people are
of such high character that they cannot be presumed to be
knowingly committing a felony." Such a position would
make gambling a crime for the uncultured and unknown,
but not for the " citizen of high character and intelligence
and great distinction." Such inconsistency in the interpretation of the laws indicates an apathy in the moral conscience which at once courts disrespect for law and threatens
us with moral dissolution. We need to open our eyes to
the situation before our apathy becomes paralysis, and develop our moral instincts by the best-known method—
healthy exercise.

So great has been our indifference that even the minions
of the law play into the hands of the law-breakers with impunity. The situation is before us: try as we will we cannot escape from the responsibility resting upon us. Shall
we seek to evade the issue by building tabernacles on the
hilltops or shall we remember that humanity lives below?

CHAPTER XIII

PROGRESS

The progress of reform in criminal procedure has not kept pace with the progress of social institutions generally. The application of science to the problem is comparatively recent, and, for the greater part of such application, it has been viewed with indifference or suspicion. Scarcely a generation has passed since men began to attribute criminality to natural causes.

Nevertheless many methods of criminal procedure now in practice or ardently advocated, are conscious or unconscious tendencies toward the somewhat radical views presented in this volume. We will consider several of them briefly.

Speaking of the progress made in the direction of amelioration of cruelty in punishment, Henderson writes:

Capital punishment has almost disappeared. Transportation seems near its end. Torture is abolished, both as a means of securing testimony and as a part of the penalty. The element of primitive revenge is gradually fading, to be displaced by a rational and dispassionate purpose of righteous retribution, accompanied by a merciful effort to reform the criminal on the way to protect society. The very names of things have changed—from " dungeon " to prison, from prison to " penitentiary " and from penitentiary to " house of correction," reformatory, reform school, industrial school and even hospitals for sick souls.[1]

[1] *Op. cit.,* p. 174.

One of the first things to shake the faith of jurists in the efficacy of the law based upon individual responsibility was the growing recognition of the fact that a great many persons brought to trial for crime were either actually insane or subject to recurring periods of insanity during which a marked tendency to crime was manifested. Many persons committed to prison for crime afterwards became raving maniacs. Judges long wrestled with the problem as to the responsibility of the insane man. Some even went so far as to assert that insanity could not be held to lessen responsibility provided the criminals were able to distinguish between right and wrong at the moment the crime was committed. The monumental work of Dr. Maudsley went far to throw light upon this perplexing subject. By his investigations it was ascertained that, in many cases, crime is an evidence of mental dissolution and the direct result of mental derangement. His work is filled with interesting examples taken from his own experience. Not the least interesting feature of his experience is the manner in which his opinions were received by the judiciary of his time. His investigations were based upon a theory set forth several years previously by a certain Dr. Pritchard in a *Treatise on Insanity*, in which it was asserted that a form of " moral insanity," consisting of an apparent lack of moral consciousness with a marked tendency to criminality, exists sometimes with an apparently unimpaired state of the intellectual faculties. This conception has been developed by Krafft-Ebing and others. The morally insane person has been identified with the instinctive or born criminal by Lombroso, Marro, Ferri, Benedikt, Hack Tuke, Kurella, and others. Of this fusion Ellis asserts there can be no doubt that the two groups in great part overlap, but a better term would be " moral imbecility " or " moral idiocy." The true insane criminal, however, need not be identified with this group but may be, as Maudsley points out, a victim of disease either hereditary or acquired.

The maniac is often undetected until his crime reveals the fact that he has long been laboring under a delusion. His crime is usually an attempt at revenge for fancied wrongs. The recent attempt of McKay upon the life of Postmaster Morgan is typical. The following is an editorial comment upon this event:

The maniac MacKay's attempt to kill Postmaster Morgan by shooting should be taken to heart as a grave warning by medical men called upon to pass upon the sanity of persons who, in fits of what is with very little plausibility described " temporary " insanity, have tried to take human life. According to the statement of MacKay's father, he inherited insanity from his mother. Some five years ago he tried to kill a Harvard student; he said the students had tormented him. It is stated that upon another occasion he tried to take a human life for fancied wrongs. He was committed to the Worcester Asylum as an insane man and escaped. He attempted to kill Postmaster Morgan because of a typical insane delusion that he had been deprived of his legal rights as to the receipt of mail matter addressed to him under a trade name he used.[1]

The desirability of attempting reformation of such cases is questioned by many. The *Times* editorial continues on this subject: " under the most liberal theory of professional ethics it may be doubted whether medical and legal service may with propriety be employed to assist any undertaking to set free a person who, according to experience and the best qualified expert opinion, would almost certainly attempt or commit further crimes of violence."

The following case given by Allison shows the wisdom of this criticism:

[1] *New York Times*, Nov. 11, 1908.

We have one man whose time expired fourteen years ago. He has committed four murders. He committed one, was imprisoned, and at the end of a short time discharged. He committed a second, went to prison, and was discharged. A third was committed and for the third time he was discharged. After the fourth he was found to be insane while undergoing sentence, committed to our custody, and his time expired fourteen years ago, but he still remains with us, a dangerous man.[1]

The recognition of the fact that certain criminals not really insane are incorrigible and should be permanently detained is another long step in the right direction. We have abundance of evidence to show that multitudes of rightly-called " born criminals " are totally irresponsible. There is a growing sentiment in favor of permanent detention as opposed to the present farcical system of proportionate punishment.

The wide spread of the reformatory idea is evidence of marked progress. It is tacitly acknowledged that crimes are due to a defective or impaired condition of the criminal but it is hoped this condition may be " reformed ". We have already criticized the principle of these reformatory institutions. Their apparent " cures," however, will keep them popular until the resultant evils manifest themselves unmistakably.

As Henderson indicates, the death penalty has almost passed, and punishment has tended to grow gradually lighter. Prison humiliations are rapidly being discarded in favor of more humane and considerate treatment. Necessary detention tends to become the reason for commitment in the place of vindictive punishment.

The growing recognition of the deleterious effects of im-

---

[1] *Care and Custody of the Insane.*

prisonment upon first offenders and the uselessness of short sentences has given rise to two devices to escape such evils by avoiding their imposition. One of these devices which has become widely practiced is the probation system. Designed especially for juveniles, but practiced often in the case of adults, it attempts to take advantage of the penitence of the culprit in order to maintain his good behavior. Instead of being remanded to prison the prisoner is discharged in the custody of an officer appointed for that special purpose to whom he must report at stated intervals for a definite time. In case he fails to report or commits a fresh crime, he is rearrested by the probation officer and turned over to the judge whereupon he is usually committed to prison. This practice has not been universally successful for several reasons, not the least important of which has been the unsatisfactory character of many probation officers. Where successful, this practice reveals the fact that the crimes corrected are not the result of criminal tendencies but largely the result of accidental circumstances.

The other of these attempts to avoid the short sentence and its degrading influences is the device known as suspended sentence. As in the case of the probation system, the prisoner is tried and found guilty, but, instead of being turned over to an officer who shall be answerable for his good behavior, he is duly sentenced by the judge who, thereupon, suspends his sentence during such time as the prisoner keeps the law. In case of violation the prisoner is rearrested and subjected to commitment or fine without trial. While beneficial in many cases of crimes of passion or accident this plan is widely used by judges to escape the necessity of numerous useless and costly imprisonments.

The practice of conditional liberation of prisoners combines the scientific practice of detention and the less scientific hope of reformation. The practice varies widely

in various localities, but the principle is the same in all.
The time of the prisoner's sentence is divided into periods
of observation. As a reward for good behavior, on the
recommendation of the best authority among his keepers,
the prisoner is set at liberty a definite period of time before
the expiration of his sentence on condition that he may be
brought back for any misconduct at any time before the expiration of his sentence, to serve the remainder of his term.

Conditional liberation was adopted in Saxony in 1862;
in the Grand Duchy of Oldenberg the same year; in
part of Switzerland in 1868; in Servia in 1869; in the German Empire in 1871; in Denmark in 1873; in the Nether-
lands in 1881; in the French Republic in 1885; in Japan in
1882; in Elmira, New York, in 1868.

The nearest approach to the system advocated in this
work is the rapidly-growing practice of imposing indeterminate sentences. The greatest hindrance to the success of
such a practice at present is the difficulty of securing officials
sufficiently expert to determine what prisoners are fit for
liberty. By this system the whole of the old theory of proportionate justice is abandoned. The prisoner is considered
unfit for society, no matter what his crime may have been
and he is committed to prison until such time as he shall be
considered fit for social rehabilitation. This method of
treatment for confirmed criminals is well presented by
Drähms. The true indeterminate sentence, he writes,

implies the permanent detention of the habitual criminal without minimum or maximum limitation, but the same to continue indefinitely, or until such time as shall be determined by
a quasi-judicial board clothed with proper authority and in-
quisitorial power to suspend the sentence upon given conditions, such release to be upon reasonable evidence shown upon
the part of the prisoner, both of his willingness and ability to

respond to the claims of society as a proper, industrious, and law-abiding citizen.[1]

Such a system has its faults and good qualities. Under present conditions it will, no doubt, restore to society many who ought never to have been imprisoned at all, while on the other hand, it will release many a clever rogue who has been able to persuade his guardians that he is thoroughly repentant and that his intentions for the future are of the best. In addition to this weakness, there remains the constant menace to society of the liberation of supposedly-cured felons who have in their nature no ability to do anything but wreak havoc upon society.

The most hopeful conclusion, however, may be drawn from this practice. It indicates an ever-growing and strengthening tendency to study the criminal to find the source of his criminality. Such study, if protracted, cannot but lead to the ultimate conclusion that the whole system of proportionate justice based upon individuality must be abandoned. Candid men will not endeavor to punish an individual because of a defective or abnormal organism of which the crime is merely an expression or indication —a natural result. Ultimately this study will lead to the condition where all remedial measures and experiments shall be tried before incarceration and only the real criminals shall be detained, and those permanently.

This work would be grossly incomplete were we to close this chapter without a brief consideration of the movement to check the constant recruiting of the criminal forces— namely, the juvenile courts. These courts have been established in many states and cities in the United States. We will take as an example the now famous juvenile court of

---

[1] *Op. cit.*, p. 365.

Denver presided over by the Hon. Ben B. Lindsey, popularly known as the father of the juvenile court.

By the laws of the state of Colorado, the jurisdiction of this court covers all cases of delinquency in which the offender is sixteen years old or under. Children are looked upon as delinquents, not criminals. In addition to ordinary delinquents violators of the compulsory education law and dependent children also fall into the hands of this court. This court has jurisdiction also over all cases against adults responsible for children. Upon it devolves also enforcement of (1) the law holding parents and others responsible for the moral delinquency of children, (2) the law holding fathers responsible for the physical support, care and maintenance of children, (3) the child labor law, (4) the law forbidding the sale of intoxicants to minors, and (5) the various statutes providing for the punishment of cruelty to children.

The court is composed of a judge, two assistants, and one chief probation officer. Cases of delinquency are reported by any person or officer to the district attorney who turns the delinquents over to the court or probation officer by whom they are brought before the judge. They are never imprisoned. Every effort is made to put the child upon his honor, and he is made to feel that the court is working for him and not against him. Whenever possible the persons responsible for the child's delinquency are summarily dealt with. After a hearing, which is a long heart-to-heart talk between the judge and the prisoner, the child is turned over to the probation officer. If necessary, he is detained in a sort of school called a " home " where he receives the best of care and necessary instruction. Judge Lindsey reports that as far as one could judge after four years of work, success was attained in 95 per cent of the cases. At the time of the report only five per cent of those brought before the court had been sent to the industrial school to be kept at the expense of the state. The record of cases tried by the criminal courts shows that in over 90 per cent of the cases the prisoners were convicted of crime and that 75 per cent of the boys over seventeen years of age were sent to state institutions or prisons.

The debasing influence upon a person of being branded a criminal at this tender age and the contaminating influence of the jails cannot be overestimated. On account of this, Judge Lindsey's great fight was against the jail. Of this struggle he writes:

The jail was not abolished without work and a fight. When the fight was on, a police commission said the boys lied to me about the corruption of the jails. I sent for the Governor of the State, the mayor of Denver, the District Attorney, President of the Council, the Police Board and a dozen ministers of the gospel to listen to the story that the boys and I could tell them. They came. I sent " Mickey " to the street for the boys and for three hours they heard a story of filth and depravity from boys of nine to fifteen years of age that was so horrible and revolting that it did seem hard to believe, yet it was so true that the Governor rose up and declared that any one who said the boys lied, lied himself. The ministers preached on it and in three days the bill was passed, signed by Governor Peabody, and the jail for little children in Denver was down and out forever. Thousands of our boys had been locked up there all day and all night entirely alone. What happened can be imagined, but they never told, because no one cared, no one knew the facts. It was not the management so much as the system itself that was all wrong.[1]

It is practically certain that all who grew up under conditions created by Judge Lindsey's court and still per-

---

[1] *Report of the Denver Juvenile Court.*

sisted in being criminals might be segregated without fear of injustice to any one. Here would be detected all who manifested a criminal propensity before the age of seventeen, and most of the others might safely be classed as "pseudo-criminals" or malefactors by sheer force of circumstances, or victims of a blundering system of repression. The success of Judge Lindsey's methods with juveniles and the redemption of some adults after incarceration are irrefutable proof that a great part of our delinquents ought never to be imprisoned at all.

CHAPTER XIV

Retrospect and Prospect

There are a few words in the English language which are used familiarly by all who speak it, which stand for common ideas and are commonly accepted. They form a part of the most casual conversation and each user supposes he is expressing himself clearly in the use of them, when, in reality, were he called upon to define them clearly, like perhaps 99 per cent of his fellows, he would be astonished to learn that there are in his mind no definite ideas to correspond with them. Fortunately he is seldom called upon to do so and the terms continue to be useful vehicles for thought transmission as long as their peculiar nature is not questioned. But when some curious soul examines such words critically, their very nature and efficiency change for him and they are no longer his willing servants. If he uses them in the new sense they do not convey his thought to his hearers, while to yield to the necessity of using their old meaning for the sake of being understood robs him of definite expression. To him, henceforth, the terms are mongrels, combining several ideas and truly expressing none. Among these are God, good, evil, truth, pleasure, and righteousness. Perhaps one of the most familiar and at the same time one of the least understood is the word progress.

To the ordinary user, progress means improvement in general. For all ordinary purposes a better meaning could not be found. Generally the term is used specifically as in the phrases " moral progress," " the progress of education," " scientific progress," and others. In these specific uses a much more definite understanding of the term is implied and it is in this implied sense that most of our current definitions are given. These definitions are apt to be colored by local conceptions, however, since the standard of measurement of the improvement is often different in different localities. Always we are hampered by our own conception of what is better or what is worse. The broader the territory and the more general the principle involved the more nearly do we approach to a real criterion of any form of progress. Thus moral progress might be clearly indicated by an increased response to a moral stimulus over a large territory. The stimulus might in itself be far below the moral standard of certain localities within the territory. In this broad sense Ward essays to measure the progress of civilization by the growth of sympathy, or in other words, " by the capacity of men for suffering representative pain." [1]

Social progress is roughly defined as the continuous progression of society in general from a lower to a higher social order. Here, of course, our criterion of progress is our conception of lower or higher orders of society. We shall never be able to escape from this difficulty entirely. Dr. Giddings' definition of progress is probably the most nearly free from this difficulty and conceives of progress as that change taking place in society whereby society as a whole is enabled to function at an ever-decreasing cost to the individuals composing it. [2] In other words, it is that change which has continued from the beginning and is still going on, which affords an ever-increasing amount of happiness to an ever-increasing number of individuals. The cause for this change, which all of us must acknowledge is continu-

[1] *Pure Sociology*, p. 346.   [2] *Unpublished Lectures.*

ally taking place, constitutes the God of the most rational as well as the most orthodox.

Contributing to this general betterment of humanity is the progress which is taking place in society's treatment of its criminals. The brief survey of this progress given in the last chapter points out a condition which gives rise to hope for the future. One can, without a great flight of imagination, look on such changes in criminal procedure as the signs of the times pointing the way to the sweeping changes that must ultimately come. But, while revealing a state of unrest and dissatisfaction on the part of our thinkers and doers with conditions that exist they show us the magnitude of the evils to be corrected and the numerous difficulties which must be overcome before these changes can be accomplished.

The probability of a speedy improvement of the situation is remote on account of these evils. So occupied have we been in looking after our individual welfare that great social interests have suffered by reason of our neglect. We have yet to learn that our individual wants and desires must be subservient to those of our group. Our brother's blood cries out from the ground little heeded by us as yet. Little that is great has been accomplished by persons who have striven for their own gratification only. Science, learning, and invention progress in the hands of their devotees; social betterment must look to enthusiasts for humanity for its progression. Little improvement can be looked for in the medical profession if the ambition of all doctors is to earn fees only, nor is the law dignified by practitioners who court skill in its manipulation for the mere sake of retainers. As Ellis writes, " both lawyers and doctors exist for the sake of society and society has the right to make certain demands upon them." Society's most urgent need is citizens who are humanitarians before they are doctors, lawyers, or merchants. The laborer who works for his pay renders an indifferent service; the excellent production is the work of him who glories in his achievement.

In a country of free institutions like ours it is a reflection upon one's self to complain of unjust laws or of indifferent legislatures. Our legislatures are our instrumentalities and our laws the expression of our sentiments in civic matters. Wherever this is not so, it is because we have allowed them to be otherwise. Our indifference in matters of legislation and in politics generally has been the direct cause of our present corrupt and unsettled conditions. Our indifference to the broad and general principles of righteousness has been responsible for the vagaries of justice that have stigmatized and continue to stigmatize our courts. Our prisons and jails have been rotting sores and pest houses in our communities because we have indifferently allowed them to be such. The politician is not hard to account for and we need not be surprised if his régime is characterized by graft. He cannot exist without it. He draws no salary but always gets rich, yet we have no one to blame for his presence but ourselves. We make his business profitable so that without salary and often without office he is well paid. The public annually pays him just as surely as it does those legitimately upon its pay-roll. But when we permit our vital social institutions to fall into the hands of the politicians, to become the spoils of party victory, the absurdity of the situation is only exceeded by its public menace. " The prison," says Drähms, " above all other corporate and civil institutions, should be above the reach of partisan machination and should in no case be classified among the prerequisites and spoils of victory in the game of politics." [1]

With our political affairs in the hands of the ring politi-

---

[1] *Op. cit.,* p. 371.

cians, our defective, dependent, and criminal classes present an additional menace because of the ease with which they can be manipulated by unscrupulous district leaders. A partial solution of the situation would be comparatively easy. Dependents and defectives who fall into the hands of the state in any way, should be disfranchised as should all confirmed criminals. Inability or unwillingness to bear the responsibilities of society warrants society in refusing to the unfit or unwilling the privilege of directing its activities. The sale of a vote and bribery should be offences incurring disfranchisement because both violate the first principles of popular government. The question of foreigners presents greater difficulties. That they are an effectual and willing instrument in the hands of the political boss has long been demonstrated by the career of Tammany Hall. Naturalization on an educational basis might help in this respect.

That immigration contributes a large share toward our defective, dependent and criminal population cannot be denied. Allison asserts that the foreign contingent among the criminally insane is particularly evident. Many persons previously inmates of prisons and asylums abroad have been helped to this country to relieve their home communities of the burden of their support.[1]

Lecky assumes that democratic institutions cannot be successful on account of the ignorance of the populace and its easy manipulation in the hands of the strong but unscrupulous personality.[2] We feel that indifference on the part of the capable is a greater menace to popular institutions than ignorance. Corruption could not exist without it. This indifference becomes criminal when it becomes so obtuse as to permit such an important institution as the courts of

---

[1] *Insanity among Criminals.*   [2] *Democracy and Liberty.*

justice to be corrupted by politics. That without a murmur from the people the arbiters of civil disputes, the highest judicial tribunals and the custodians of the social well-being should be appointed by a successful ringster from amongst his henchmen on the basis of their or their friends' ability to corrupt voters or supply campaign funds, is certainly the most severe indictment conceivable against free institutions. With truth Allen writes, " we have expressed little interest in the character of the acts of a magistrate who flips a coin to decide whether a man should be turned loose upon society or imprisoned." [1]

In connection with the corruption of the courts, the duplicity of the police force in large cities presents one of the greatest difficulties in the way of the suppression of crime. Because of this corruption gambling and prostitution exist in most flagrant violation of law and with the tacit acknowledgment of the authorities that they cannot be stopped. Our repressive system presents the marvelous spectacle of a net which catches the little offenders and lets the big ones escape. This fact leads Henderson to write:

We would avoid indiscriminate reflection; yet the fact remains that there is scarcely a city in the United States where the saloon, the gambling hell and the brothel, each and all in contravention of law and ordinance, do not carry forward the demoralizing and destructive work under the immediate observation and immediate personal knowledge of the police, while at the same time the honest but hilarious newsboy or bootblack, in giving vent to boyish propensities, is rudely dragged through the public thoroughfare, hustled into the dark and dirty station house, forced into association with the idle and vicious, arraigned, tried and convicted in the police court, where he is made a spectacle of disgrace in the eyes of those

[1] *Op. cit.*, p. 184.

who study law and derive their ideas of public justice from such proceedings.[1]

" Dark streets," writes Allen, " and sleepy patrolmen make work for many gaolers."

What the public does with the offender and not the number of offenders apprehended is the test of efficiency in preventing crime. An increase in arrests is not a sure sign of increasing criminality: it may mean increasing blackmail; it may mean the approach of election; it often means increased vigilance and efficiency on the part of the police. The police, however, are not entirely to blame. Nine-tenths of their prisoners would be released on some pretext or other if taken to court, and the arrest of certain well-known violators protected by the political machine would mean the instant loss of a job. To clean any section of the correctional machinery would be a useless waste of time and means. The whole mechanism needs renovation throughout. I am not sure we do not need a new plant.

In the light of these conditions the fact becomes evident that the indifference of the people is the greatest hindrance to progress either in rectifying evils or correcting defects. " Without a well-defined public sentiment," writes Drähms, " properly educated and trained, all attempted reform is apt to fall dead born, or is at least but spasmodic and weak."

Our indifference in itself becomes criminal. " Few crimes in the calendar," says Allen, " offend so greatly against moral and social laws as do good people who fail to assure themselves that through their system of police, juries, judges, and penal institutions they are not adding to the sum total of human wretchedness." " It is a hard thing," says Seymour, " to draw an indictment against a criminal

[1] *Op. cit.*, p. 203.

which is not an indictment of the community in which he
has lived."

Our very business seems to be shifting to a questionable
basis. " Get rich honestly if possible—but get rich," is not
the foundation upon which great characters are built. The
excuse that the money one .might obtain by questionable
methods will be gotten by some one else by the same methods does not free one from the moral obligation of integrity.
" It is genetically true," writes Dr. Giddings, "as it is ideally
true, that righteousness exalteth a nation." [1] It is also true
that " sin is a reproach to any people." Drähms declares
that the " selfishness that will force a conflict upon labor
for purely selfish purposes, at the expense of human happiness, is fully as anti-social as any isolated act of overt law-
lessness born in the throes of private necessity."

The wide spread of public sentiment against alcoholism
throughout Europe and America is a most gratifying condition to the observer of social progress. " The decrease
of the use of alcoholic drinks," says Drähms, " must ever
remain the aim of all criminal legislation, as well as of
moral and social reform. Intemperance is the chief source
of crime, both directly and indirectly. It affects alike the
occasional, the habitual, and the congenital criminal."

New York's anti-gambling victory followed by that of
Louisiana and the present hopeful fight in California are
signs of moral progress. Several recent verdicts against
grafting politicians and officeholders, embezzling bankers
and swindling corporations also tend to confirm the belief
in the integrity of the people along broad moral lines.

We still contribute to crime in many unthinking and
unnoticed ways. Debauchery of the public press in sen-

---

[1] *Sociology, a lecture delivered at Columbia University,* Feb. 26,
1908, p. 43.

sational portrayal of murder cases, divorce suits, *etc.,* for pecuniary gain is little short of criminal. Note, for instance, the frequency of "brain-storms" occurring throughout the country after the Thaw fiasco and the frequent resorts to the "unwritten law" as a defense for crimes many of which occur as a result of the debauchery and domestic wretchedness exploited by the daily papers. Yet yellow journals exist because such sheets are profitable, and profitable because they are eagerly read by the masses. They will disappear as soon as the demand for them ceases It is a simple case of economics. The publishers stay within the law. The fault is in the law and in us who are responsible for it. Obscene literature and pictures and flaming posters testify to the fact that there is a market for lewd publications and that questionable shows bring crowded houses.

A great deal of our responsible and irresponsible activity in regard to our defective, dependent, and criminal classes has been characterized by sentimentalism and devoid of common sense. As Henderson suggests, any community can have as much pauperism and criminality as it cares to pay for.

We have, no doubt, expected too much of humanity. When we take into consideration the vast period of time during which it struggled up through animalism and savagery to barbarism, and the period almost as long when it rose through the various stages of barbarism to the lowest form of civilization, the few thousand years since the beginning of our present civilization seem but a moment in comparison. The real marvel is that we have accomplished so much. It is not strange that the rapid progress of the past few centuries has developed vagaries. There are few of our evils that are not remnants of outgrown institutions or the overstepping of present goods. Our greatest social evils are but the survival of once legitimate practices. We could not expect the whole of society to progress at the same rate. Some individuals lag behind and cling to practices abandoned or outlawed by the bulk of society; others receive an unbalanced portion of the progressive impulse and we have our vagaries, our freaks. Thus sentimentalism is humanitarianism without the guidance of reason—unlimited sympathy with a dearth of science. The well-balanced individual is the goal of evolution.

Nor can we expect this thin veneer of civilization to restrain effectually the fundamental barbarism of contemporary society or curb its still more fundamental savagery or control that slumbering animalism, rooted in the primal instincts of hunger and of sex, which is beneath the other characteristics of a human being and more potent than them all. The individual consciousness, the rare product of our highest development, is easily submerged beneath our barbarian and savage instincts under appeals which rouse those latent forces. This has led many writers to assert that beneath the veneer of altruism in the masses is an inherent love of blood and vengeance. Outrage the moral conceptions of our highest stage of development and the mass instantly reverts to a lower one and we have the mob, the riot, the lynching, and murder. Under privation alone however do we revert to animalism. The reversion is near or remote in proportion to the degree of progress attained by each individual.

That in the course of this slow but steady progress there should be an apparent or real retrograde movement can be accounted for in one way only. We have permitted our rapidly-developing humanitarian sentiments, our altruism, to interfere with the natural selective process which guided our faltering steps so far on our upward way. This process was cruel to individuals but beneficent to the race. For

this reason much progress had to be made before the individual could be taken into consideration at all; and when
at last individuality began to emerge it was with terrific cost
to the race that it did so.   As long as the weaklings and
the infirm fell by the wayside without a murmur, the general progress of human development continued unchecked.
When those who fell out of the ranks cried out against
their lot, a menace to progress arose but no actual hindrance; but when this cry for aid first struck a responsive
chord in some stronger breast, the individual as such was
born, but the progress of human development received a
serious blow.   The individual who first paused to lend a
helping hand marked the birth of humanity but doomed the
race to ultimate degeneration unless the natural result of
his violation of the law of survival is counteracted by some
other influence.

A long reprieve has been granted from this doom.   During this time humanity has been responsible for the development of the best that is in man.   Without it we would
have remained beasts or savages.   But now, in the
height of humanity's triumphs, the unchangeable law demands the fulfilment of its decree.   Wise law said only
the best must survive; we have done our utmost to save and
perpetuate the worst, with the result that all are now threatened with degeneration.   The objects of our pity have
multiplied exceedingly; they fill our hospitals, our almshouses, our asylums, our prisons and our slums.   They
marry into and corrupt our best stocks so that our whole
social body is contaminated.

Recent writers have appreciated this situation and have
cried out against it, apparently in vain, yet all are hopeful
of the future.   One of the most marked characteristics of
present man is his confidence in his own ingenuity.   In the
presence of the inevitable he still hopes for some means of

escape, and gloomy as the present outlook is, there is one certain way out—a way that squares us with the law. The natural selective process which was interfered with so long ago must be replaced by an artificial one, no less effectual, which will safeguard the vitality of the race without interfering with its humanity. Receive your weaklings as a charge from Heaven if you will, keep them in all kindness and mercy until they die a natural death, but see to it that the spirit of the law of selection is enforced—that they do not multiply their kind. Since a large part of our criminals and defectives and dependents are born of these classes, this method would reduce the numbers of them in a single generation to those who appear as the result of the struggle for existence, who in turn should become public wards of the social system which gave them birth.

" It is utopian," writes Allen, " to expect that the time will ever come when individuals shall cease to offend against society. It is not utopian, however, to look forward to a time when society shall cease to offend against individuals either before or after those individuals are convicted of crime." [1]

It is not pessimistic to assert that we shall never be without our defective, dependent, and criminal classes. As long as the struggle for existence and moral progress continue, men will continue to lose out in the struggle or fall below the moral standard; but their number will grow less year by year as the humanitarian and moral standards become identified and more and more pervade the great bulk of society. As our wards, the criminals, grow fewer their power to injure society will grow less. The type of manhood and womanhood developed under these conditions will be such as to lessen the severity of the struggle for existence

[1] *Efficient Democracy*, p. 203.

and fewer will fall by the way. The distinction between sin and crime will cease to be made, for everyone will see that anything which hurts him must ultimately hurt his brother. In the state where this conception reigns, the ideal now hoped for will be attained—the association where perfect justice has become perfect science and both are synonymous with perfect sympathy.

La Bibliothèque
Université d'Ottawa
Echéance

The Library
University of Ottawa
Date due

FEB 19 '77